MENTAL HEALTH AWARENESS TO REDUCE ANXIETY AND STRESS

Deal with Stress, Anxiety, Burnout, And Disorders Even During Crisis

Mental Heath Awareness to Reduce Anxiety and Stress: Deal with Stress, Anxiety, Burnout, and Disorders Even During Crisis

By Alexandria Sparks

ISBN: 9798723268616

First printing edition 2021.

Gutel Leather
1201 24th St
B110-371
Bakersfield CA 93301

Table of Contents

INTRODUCTION

<u>What Can You Do If You Have Anxiety in Your Brain?</u>

"I'm not sure I want to live if I have to keep feeling this way." It is a common comment I hear from anxiety sufferers. They may say it casually or dramatically, but they all agree that if anxiety symptoms are going to dominate their lives, they don't seem worth living. What is it about anxiety that makes people who are otherwise high-functioning so desperate to getaway? The feelings of impending doom, dread, or fear can be extremely overwhelming. They are, in reality, the same feelings that a person would have if the worst were to happen.

Anxiety is rampant in this millennium. A panic attack affects up to a third of the United States population at some stage in their lives. According to the Anxiety Disorder Association of America's website, 40 million Americans suffer from anxiety disorders. Those who suffer from anxiety are three to five times more likely to seek medical treatment and six times more likely to be treated for mental disorders than those who do not suffer from anxiety. People who are panicked or fearful are frequently compelled to seek immediate relief from medicine, but this prevents them from learning more about what is causing their anxiety or finding other strategies for reducing anxiety. Medication, which is considered the first-line treatment for anxiety by insurance and drug providers, is losing public favor when people learn that it has adverse side effects and that their symptoms reappear when they avoid taking it.

The good news is that a recent neurobiology study has forever altered medical care for anxiety disorders. Structural and functional issues cause anxiety in the brain. It means that people have a lot of control over how they use their minds to alter them. Medication is only one of the options available; people can also reduce their anxiety by making lifestyle changes. People can alleviate their anxiety by altering aspects of their lifestyle, thought, and actions, which is just one of many choices.

<u>Types of Anxiety and Anxiety Symptoms</u>

<u>The anxiety clusters are divided into three main groups: panic disorder, widespread anxiety disorder, and social anxiety disorder.</u>

- Panic disorder is characterized by a high level of physical arousals, such as a racing pulse, hyperventilation, dizziness, nausea, and other symptoms.

- Generalized anxiety disorder is characterized by six months or more of constant concern about everyday activities, robbing daily life of fun, impairing concentration, and causing a sense of dread or doom. This condition can be seen in children, especially tho1se concerned about their academic performance (which is different from school refusal).

- Social anxiety disorder (also known as "social phobia") is defined by a person's avoidance of environments and events that cause them to flush, shake, or sweat and make them feel nervous. School phobia in young children can lead to social anxiety, so it's important to determine what's causing it and treat it. This book's methods can be used to treat the physical, cognitive (mental), and behavioral effects of any of these conditions. As a result, rather than concentrating on diagnosis, this book will concentrate on symptom clusters.

- The nervous system. Negative physical arousal, such as the terror of panic, the flushing, sweating, the humiliated look of social anxiety, and the agitation of people who are too "wired" and nervous, are all physical signs. The methods described in Part II of this book will help you control these symptoms.

- Nervous feelings. Overactivity in the brain causes mental stress and the mental anguish of rumination and worry, which leads to cognitive symptoms. An anxious mind is caused by a brain that won't stop thinking distressing thoughts. Part III's strategies provide suggestions for relaxing an agitated mind.

- Anxiety-related behavior. The avoidance behaviors of the panicked and socially insecure individual and the complex and subtler avoidance habits of the general worrier are behavioral symptoms. Part IV's strategies focus on modifying nervous behavior, which is a common result of panic and anxiety.

The three clusters of symptoms are caused by activity in various parts of the brain. When something in the brain isn't functioning properly, it impacts how a person feels, thinks, and behaves. Techniques that use the brain to alter the brain can regulate physical, emotional, and behavioral anxiety symptoms. Anxiety can be slowed and stopped using the techniques in this book. Science will now demonstrate why they function. We've learned more and more about how consistent application of anxiety management strategies can relax an anxious brain since the advent of brain-imaging in science. When you know which strategies to try and how to make them work, you will achieve a relaxed mind.

MANAGING ANXIETY IN THE BODY PART 1

People who have panic disorder are terrified of the actual sensation of being afraid. They never want to have another panic attack because the experience's severity is so painful and frightening. Your heart races, your breathing is fast and shallow, your chest hurts, and it is possible that you feel sweltered, sick-mouthed, shaky, or tingly unpleasant. The panic disorder develops when people fear getting another panic attack and tend to limit their behaviors. Understandably, you'd never want to suffer a panic attack. They are both physically and psychologically painful. They are not, however, lethal, as I will demonstrate later. Many variables can be regulated to reduce the frequency and duration of panic attacks.

<u>You can experience the following symptoms if you have the panic disorder:</u>

- ✓ Rapid heart rate
- ✓ Hyperventilation or shallow breathing

- ✓ Nausea and vomiting
- ✓ A tingling sensation
- ✓ Ear ringing
- ✓ A lump in your throat
- ✓ Feeling dizzy

Physical signs of anxiety are also present in other forms of anxiety. People who suffer from generalized anxiety (the worrywarts among us) have a lot of tension-related issues. A few examples include temporomandibular joint (T.M.J.) or jaw joint pain, neck pain and headaches, and stomach and gastrointestinal pain. Furthermore, the physical sensation of acute anxiety—the physical feeling that something is seriously wrong—is excruciatingly painful. Managing the body is critical for those with generalized anxiety to experience less physical discomfort while also reducing anxiety.

If a person has generalized anxiety, you will see some of the following symptoms:

- ✓ Sense of doom or dread
- ✓ Achiness

- ✓ Muscle tension
- ✓ Agitation or restlessness

Sufferers of social anxiety tremble at the prospect of others perceiving them as fearful. Social anxiety distress is the focus of Macdonald's (2005) study, which shows that mental pain can be felt physically. Flushing, sweating, heart palpitations, and quivering muscles or voices are all temporary symptoms—uncomfortable but not long-lasting if you can avoid the fear of others' attention.

There is also evidence that the unease of knowing that someone will notice the symptoms hurt and constant anxiety can prominently hold the pain in your thoughts. Our emotional distress abstract images make us feel pain. People with social pressures appear to be overly sensitive to their own emotions and activities externally (Aron, 1996; Lonegan & Philips, 2001; McNally, 2002). It causes more physical discomfort than the outward symptoms of their fear.

Social anxiety sufferers may experience:

- ✓ Flushing or blushing
- ✓ Sweating
- ✓ Quivering muscles
- ✓ Quivering voice
- ✓ Heart palpitations

These symptoms can be present in a person, and their severity varies significantly from one person to the next. For several people suffering from anxiety, there is a vicious cycle in which physical arousal triggers anxiety and anxiety triggers physical arousal. Interrupting this mechanism reduces arousal and reduces the frequency and severity of anxiety symptoms.

Get A Medical Examination Before Beginning Psychotherapy.

There are far too many physical causes of anxiety to list them all here, and doing so will only make you more nervous. Even if you've always been worried, anxious, or shy, getting a medical check for heart, hormonal, or blood-sugar problems is vital if your symptoms have recently escalated. Changes in thyroid function, for example, can cause anxiety, and mitral valve prolapse can cause panic. The way your brain absorbs neurotransmitters can be affected by estrogen and progesterone changes, and as neurotransmitters change, so do physical stimuli, mood, thinking, and actions. Since this book's approaches do not solve the underlying medical condition causing your anxiety, you will have limited success with them. When people visit their family doctor or go to the E.R. for a panic attack, they are usually given a battery of tests that come out negative (i.e., show no physical problems). Their signs are said to be unrelated to any medical condition. They seek therapy out of desperation. These individuals can find it difficult to accept that therapeutic strategies may help them control physical symptoms. They conclude that if no medical attention is needed, they must not have had any physical signs at all. Anxiety is, however, physically felt. When you're sure no illness or medical condition is causing your symptoms, the methods I'll teach you will make a huge difference.

This segment discusses techniques for calming anxiety's physiology (physical symptoms). The brain, which is, after all, a part of the physical body, is managed by relaxing the body, according to research (Amen, 1998; Benson, 1975; Childre, 1999; Gallo, 2005; Schwartz, 2005). Physical changes can have a considerable impact on how people think and behave when it comes to anxiety. The brain's physical organ reacts to both external and internal stressors. Ringing phones can be as upsetting as consuming the wrong foods. Whatever is bothering your brain can manifest itself in your physiology, emotions, and behavior.

Energy therapies, eye movement desensitization, and reprocessing neurofeedback, heart math, and biofeedback are only a few strategies for controlling the anxious body. However, these methods necessitate the use of specialists. Fortunately, there are several tried-and-true techniques that you can use entirely on your own.

This segment describes four that will assist you in adjusting negative arousing intakes, reducing stressors and the effects of stress, and calming down the body once it begins to experience anxious symptoms:

- ✓ **<u>Technique 1:</u>** Change Your intake
- ✓ **<u>Technique 2:</u>** Breath
- ✓ **<u>Technique 3:</u>** Practice Mindfulness with Shifting Awareness
- ✓ **<u>Technique 4:</u>** Relax

These four strategies relax the movement of the brain and thus excite the body. The quieter your brain, the less you experience painful physical stimuli of all kinds.

<u>Technique 1: Change Your Intake</u>

Whatever you consume must be processed by your body. Your body (including your brain as an organ) responds to chemicals or high environmental stimuli to restore balance in all your systems. One of the costs of being out of control is anxiety symptoms.

Changing your diet is the first step in calming your nervous body. Changing your diet may involve eliminating foods or medications that cause anxiety, as well as increasing your intake of stimuli and reducing the demands that stress your brain and body.

Technique 1 is one which you can begin to do today. It will make a significant difference in calming your anxiety.

LIMIT C.A.T.S.

Caffeine, alcohol, tobacco, sugar, and sweetener are all abbreviated as C.A.T.S. According to a study, these substances play a role in triggering physical distress, and when a person's intake of these substances is decreased, the body becomes less anxious right away. <u>Knowing how restricting your intake of C.A.T.S. will help you decide whether limiting your intake of one or all of these substances is a good first step can help you decide whether limiting your intake of one or all of these substances is a good first step.</u>

Avoiding caffeine can be a decision that doesn't seem a brainer until you realize that you don't like coffee, tea, or soft drinks with caffeine. It does not bode well. But you do not know how you are affected by these caffeinated substances. Research has shown that a person's genetic make-up appears to cause caffeine intake outside of blue panic (Alsene, Deckert, Sand, & de Wit, 2003; Nardi, 2007). Even relatively small levels of caffeine can cause panic. A young man who saw me as he felt fear every day and sometimes significant panic attacks that led him to the emergency room said that his panic was caused by caffeine, as he had too little to eat. In the mornings, he only drank one cup of daily coffee, and in the afternoons, he rarely drank a soda. He reduced the frequency and intensity of his panic attacks with other techniques, but after another terrifying panic attack, he decided to give up caffeine completely. He could immediately tell the difference, and he didn't have another major panic attack. Caffeine, on the other hand, does more than trigger anxiety. Worriers, who may have generalized anxiety, are usually physically tense, and caffeine's effect on the nervous system may raise their stress levels (Fisone, Borgkvist, & Usiello, 2004; Fredholm, Bättig, Holmén, Nehlig, & Zvartau, 1999). Caffeine affects people who experience flushing, sweating, and shakiness as a result of their social anxiety. They become more likely to feel anxiety symptoms that they do not want the world to see by increasing their nervous system's arousal with caffeine.

Caffeine is generally a contributor to any form of anxiety. Notice the quantities of caffeine you can use, such as soda, coffee, tea, chocolate and energy drinks, and tablets, in everyday items. The milligrams of caffeine can be found easily on the Internet in these items. People vary greatly in intolerance to caffeine; some of them can't even drink small amounts of caffeine; however, you'll quickly find your limits and change your dosage accordingly if you keep up with your mood, tension, and anxiety changes.

- ❖ *<u>Alcohol</u>*

Many people use alcohol to relieve stress, cope with anxiety, and prevent uncomfortable emotional states daily. A moderate amount of alcohol can cause a relaxed state of mind or body quickly and momentarily. The effect of alcohol on the nervous body, however, is more complicated than it seems. Anxious people are more likely than those who do not consume alcohol in larger quantities or more frequently. People may drink more alcohol when they are under a lot of stress, such as during a divorce and challenging projects involving long hours of work or caring for a sick family member. All of these conditions can make relaxation or sleep difficult, and alcohol can aid.

Alcohol can also help with social anxiety. It can help a person relax when confronted with a social requirement, such as attending an office party.

People use alcohol to get rid of unpleasant emotions or achieve the states of relaxation they crave, and in doing so, they unintentionally create a more significant anxiety issue. While alcohol can temporarily help people relax, it is a powerful anxiety-inducing substance.

As alcohol leaves the body after being detoxified by the liver, it causes nerves to become irritated. People who have a couple of drinks before bedtime may find it easier to become drowsy and fall asleep, but they often wake up halfway through the night and cannot return to sleep. It is because alcohol causes the nervous system to become agitated. Suppose you don't want to give up alcohol altogether. In that case, the safest way to avoid waking up in the middle of the night is to limit alcohol intake to earlier in the evening so that this process of detoxification is completed before going to bed.

The best approach is to use herbal teas at bedtime to achieve sleepiness without recovery (such as kava, camomile, catnip, lemon balm, hops, and valerian). The herbs in these teas help to relax the mind and encourage sleep, with no unpleasant side effects in the morning. Always check how herbal substances communicate with each other and any other drugs you're taking before using them. Even though the F.D.A. does not control these substances, they can interact with or counteract the effects of other herbs or medications you are taking.

The hangover effect, which occurs when too much alcohol is consumed, is a more apparent issue with alcohol and anxiety. Excessive alcohol consumption is popular among young people. Binge drinking is prevalent, and it usually begins in late adolescence. It is not "social drinking," and it has implications that should be seen as a risk factor for addiction and anxiety, all of which can grow due to excessive alcohol consumption. When alcohol addiction is present, it must be treated separately from anxiety management;

addiction will not go away simply because they can handle their anxiety.

The aim of analyzing alcohol use in the context of an anxious body is to figure out how it causes anxiety rather than alleviates it. The irritated brain is primed to feel more anxiety and fear as it attempts to recover from alcohol consumption. Maintaining an anxiety or panic journal is one way to monitor the effects of alcohol on your body. Keep track of how much you drank the night before and how anxious you were the next day. For a few months, keeping this journal will reveal a great deal about how alcohol affects the body.

❖ *<u>Tobacco</u>*

Tobacco use has so many negative consequences that it's difficult to imagine why anyone would use it. People do, however, smoke. Tobacco is calming to those that use it, and the behavior associated with it leads to that relaxation.

The act of lighting a cigarette, pipe, or cigar, or chewing tobacco, is also strongly associated with creating a space of relaxation and isolation from tension. The smoker can step out, relax, think, and soothe himself. An announcement that he must stop smoking is the fastest way to make an anxious person even more nervous.

Tracking the relationship between anxiety symptoms and tobacco use is a more robust approach. Dizziness, tingling, shortness of breath, or just the nagging belief that you shouldn't be smoking due to the health risks are all anxiety-inducing consequences of smoking. You can't know how smoking can affect others unless you track their reactions.

You'll be able to tell if your tobacco use is linked to the severity of your anxiety pretty quickly. When one of my clients recently quit smoking, he confirmed that the intense feeling of fear made him think he would have a panic attack vanished instantly. He believes it was because he was ashamed of himself for smoking every cigarette but didn't want to admit it. Several of my clients told me that smoking reduces their anxiety but then increases it. Before you light the cigarette, do some diaphragmatic breathing or one of the fast breathing relaxers if you are working on controlling anxiety's physical sensations. These exercises might make you feel less tempted to pick up a cigarette in the first place by reducing your underlying anxiety.

Sugar and Sweeteners

Sugar and non-nutritive sweeteners trigger a slew of anxiety-inducing issues. For starters, sugar may have anxiety-like effects in hypoglycemic people. Hypoglycemia means low blood sugar. Low blood sugar symptoms (such as sweating, flushing, nausea, and shakiness) are somewhat similar to much of the physical sensations that cause anxiety. Like most health conditions that go through a fad of being over-diagnosed, hypoglycemia was once blamed for various physical and mental issues. According to Andrew Weil (1998), unstable blood sugar is rare because the brain relies on a steady supply of blood sugar, and the body has a variety of mechanisms to keep levels within a safe range. However, some people have hypoglycemia, and some people are more vulnerable to the effects of blood sugar fluctuations. Many people who suffer from anxiety have more severe physical symptoms and pay more attention to them than others. When a person with hypoglycemia eats foods that quickly convert to sugar (For instance, simple carbohydrates such as a donut or a plate of pasta), their blood sugar level rises quickly. The blood sugar level drops rapidly after that, resulting in symptoms that resemble anxiety. Consuming complex carbohydrates rather than simple carbohydrates, balancing your meals with protein, and avoiding caffeine are all effective ways to combat this issue.

Since the research on aspartame's adverse effects is problematic, non-nutritive sweeteners, especially aspartame, are complicated. Many studies show no exact adverse reactions to these substances, but others offer a connection between aspartame consumption and increased anxiety.

Aspartame has been shown to directly affect nerves by altering the myelin sheath (the nerves' protective covering) (Blaylock, 2004; Muller, Peterson, Sonnewald, & Unsgard, 1995; Walton, 1988). Furthermore, a significant number of anecdotal reports citing adverse reactions to aspartame, including those from my clients, recommend that aspartame be eliminated to monitor any role it could play in causing anxiety or panic symptoms.

In the field of non-nutritional sweeteners in general, the wisest option might be the prudent use of sugar. Still, if you need to stop sugar entirely since you are sugar-sensitive, a non-chemical, non-nutritious stevia sweetener is widely available in food shops. Chemicals in our foods tax our bodies' ability to absorb them and many people with nervous bodies respond to aspartame and other chemicals. Reducing chemical intake, in general, is a good idea, and removing aspartame is an obvious way to do so. Keep track of your anxiety levels after consuming aspartame or sugar, and if you experience a rise in symptoms, it's time to cut down or stop using it altogether.

Create Demand Delays

The need for an immediate response to communication has generated a new category of stress in our current culture. Many of us are used to the notion that we must answer the phone immediately, answer an email, or send a fax instead of a "snail mail" message. You may be among those with high drive—many energy to keep up with, regardless of your activities—so that you may not be aware of the extent of the demand for contact. Whenever the machine or phone tells us that a message is waiting, our brains register an alert. As a request for consideration, the amygdala hears a thing. The warning is only calmed, and if we do not respond at once, mental energy is needed to push away the urge to react.

Hearing another person's phone ring causes mental (and therefore physical) tension. All of our commu1nication-related technology has instilled in us an artificial "on-call" state that we must maintain daily— a constant state of alertness and readiness to react quickly. Email, voicemail, text messages, instant messages, and other communication forms are in high demand. Expectations at work exacerbate this feeling. "Oh?" says the manager, his forehead furrowed. "Didn't you get the message? I sent you an email at 9 p.m. last night informing you that the meeting this morning will begin an hour earlier than scheduled." It's implied that you can check in with work at all hours of the day. Many employers require employees to review emails on weekends, and healthcare professionals, especially mental health professionals, frequently need to be on call at all times, often for days at a time. The stress of staying alert is subtle but persistent, and it contributes significantly to physical tension.

To see how "answer demand" tension affects you, it may be a good idea to minimize it. Mike, a client who joked that his Bluetooth earpiece was surgically inserted, misplaced his phone on a business trip. It felt beautiful not being able to answer the phone or respond to emails while spending the day with his client, he realized. He was attentive to the customer, concentrating on his work, and believed he did a better job than if he had been listening to the rings and dings of his web-enabled phone. He was anxious without the phone, but he could push the fear aside because he had no options and felt calmer on the job than he had in a long time. And on the way home, he felt happier because he could listen to music instead of returning calls. Establish a reasonable test period to observe this because changing your practice of responding to communication demands may temporarily increase anxiety before providing relief. Turning off touch makes you nervous about what you're missing, as any "crackberry" user (someone addicted to checking voicemail and email) can testify. You'll have to get used to the feeling of being disconnected.

Limit your availability to answer the phone, email messages, text messages, faxes, pager calls, and other communication forms to reduce the effect of this tension, and see how your anxiety level improves. Creating demand delays is what this is known as. Choose one of the following suggestions to experiment with for at least a week to see which one works best for you. The ultimate goal is to have complete control over when you react to your technological demands, but start small. Before, during, and after your technology-free period, rate your anxiety on a 0-10 scale (with ten being high).

- Don't check your email until at least an hour into the workday. Next, try to get some job done.

- Check voicemail during the day when it is most convenient for you to take messages and answer calls. (You may want to include this detail in your outgoing notification, so callers know when to expect a callback.)

- Switch off all ringing and dinging devices when you're working.

- Turn off all ringing devices at home, including mobile phones, when you eat. Make mealtimes a call-free zone.

- When you go into a restaurant, leave your phone in the car or, at the very least, set the ringer to silent (not vibrate) so that your focus is entirely on your meal and your companions. (Exercise the same caution in movies, theaters, assemblies, churches, and lectures.)

- If you have a pager for work, make sure you turn it off when you're not on call and don't allow anyone to use it to contact you when you're not on call.

- Separate personal and work-related phone numbers to a certain extent, so you can choose not to answer the work phone without missing calls from family or friends. Often, don't take job calls on your time.

- When you're asked to bring a machine home or work from home, make sure you and your boss agree on the exact hours you're going to work. Except during those hours, don't respond to work messages. Your employer would not be able to prevent you from working nonstop; you must set the limits.

Track the effect of contact requests and how they affect your level of anxiety. It can be seen as anxiety or alertness instead of nervousness. It is also helpful to track how concerned it makes you move away from the availability of contact. Both versions of anxiety will keep the brain revived and ready to worry about apparently unrelated problems. One way to rate strain and how its levels shift when attempting to create such contact borders is to create demand delays and monitor its effects.

Lower Stimulation Intake

At work, taking a break from high-stimulation conditions can be highly beneficial in reducing stress (Schaubroeck & Ganster, 1993). While people do not often report feeling depressed due to working in an open office, their bodies display the effects of continuously trying to filter out the noise, with stress hormone levels higher than those in less noisy workplaces (Evans & Johnson, 2000). These types of breaks from being on-call can be lifesavers for people who are hypersensitive to high levels of stimuli, reducing stress and anxiety levels (Aron, 1996).

If you aren't aware of the effects of stimulation in your atmosphere, you might need to take breaks even if you don't feel obligated. The more alert you are, the more the world affects you, so taking a break from stimuli will result in more relaxed physiology.

At least every 90 minutes at work, take one of these breaks:

- ✓ Take a look outside for a moment.

- ✓ Spend some time outdoors, even if it's only a couple of minutes away.
- ✓ Have a photo of your favorite people or places on hand, and when you look at it, feel deep gratitude and love.
- ✓ Walk down the hall, drink water, or go to the bathroom, even though you don't need to, just to get some fresh air out of your desk.
- ✓ Take a 2-minute mental break.

It is a fantastic experience for people of all ages to participate in. Close your eyes and visualize a favorite location. Then go over what you saw and felt in each of your five senses. It will be about 2 minutes after you have set the scene, and you can return to the present with the feeling that you have taken a short break.

People experience stress in a variety of settings, including those outsides of work. Too much stimulation in the classroom, cafeteria, or school hallways may cause students to become grumpy or overexcited. Many parents want to take their children outside to play after spending the day with them in the home, but those responsive to stimuli must prevent anxiety-inducing stress. Shopping (particularly in malls), commuting on congested streets by car or public transportation, attending conferences with a large number of people and new knowledge, or being exposed to noise, fluorescent lighting, or other types of environmental irritants can all lead to the need for a stimulus break. It can be extremely beneficial to minimize the amount of time you spend in circumstances that are too stimulating. Take time out during the shopping day to sit down for lunch or a cup of tea. If the house is too crowded, take a break in a quiet space. Take time after situations that stimulate you to calm down your body if you find yourself getting irritable, exhausted, frustrated, or nervous. Rest, read, listen to music, take a nap in a peaceful place, breathe, or engage in a low-intensity exercise.

It's also necessary to take breaks between activities to allow your nervous system to rest and recharge. As a result, make sure that rest and quiet are a part of your post-party plans, and you'll find that the fun will be much more enjoyable. Make changes between tasks to allow your mind to relax and refocus. Chaotic environments stress people who are susceptible to overstimulation. People who are highly energetic and have a basal ganglia-generated desire to get things done do not need as much time as those who are more influenced by stimulation, but they do need the change. Transitions are crucial for keeping the drive level concentrated and, as a result, less stressful. Before returning to work, make sure you relax and prepare yourself after a significant event, such as a holiday. Make sure you've finished the previous task before moving on to the next.

<u>There are many different ways to take a break in general. For example:</u>

- ✓ Find a quiet place to sit and do something relaxing, such as reading, meditating, or just breathing.

✓ Take a break from the stimulation, even if it's only for 15 minutes.

✓ Take a bath or splash cold water on your hands while slowly exhaling.

✓ Relax by listening to soothing songs.

✓ Play a video game that requires all of your attention for a few minutes.

✓ If you're an artistic person, devote some time to painting, needlework, or playing an instrument alone.

✓ If necessary, take a break from the screen and go outside to look at the trees or gardens.

✓ If you can't leave the house, consider focusing on the most crucial aspect of the task at hand, then refocusing to shut out the distracting stimuli.

All of the following will help you lower your stimulation intake.

✓ During the day, take frequent breaks. Don't miss workouts just because you aren't stressed right now.

- ✓ Spend as little time as possible in overstimulating environments like shopping malls or sporting events. After significant incidents, take time off or alone.
- ✓ Concentrate on something that needs concentration but is not demanding, such as playing an instrument or needlework.
- ✓ Make changes between exciting events like school and an after-school social gathering.
- ✓ Provide time for relaxation and organization between significant events, such as a holiday and your return to work. Disorganized environments stress people who are susceptible to overstimulation.
- ✓ If you are unable to escape physically, take mental breaks.

<u>Increase Intake Of Nutritious Foods</u>

The nutrients in the food you consume help your brain produce neurotransmitters. And while you're sleeping, the majority of your brain cells and neurotransmitters are generated. When you are sleeping, the brain requires a protein from animal or plant sources (Delgado et al., 1994; Golberg, 1997), and the digestive process takes 12 to 15 hours for the proteins to reach the brain (DesMaisons, 1998). Another explanation why eating a healthy breakfast is a brilliant idea! Eat protein three times a day, but just 3 or 4 ounces per serving, to ensure protein availability during the night.

That portion is about the size of a card deck.

You need vitamins to ensure that your brain works properly and produces the requisite neurotransmitters (Amen, 2003; DesMasions, 1998; Weil, 1998). Food is the best source of nutrients, and vitamin supplements will help if you are deficient in some areas. Keep in mind that calories and nutrients are not synonymous. When it comes to brain well-being, what you eat is much more important than how much you eat. Folic acid, found in dark green vegetables like spinach, is needed for the production of serotonin (Delgado et al., 1994; Wolfersdorf, Maier,

Froscher, Laage, & Straub, 1994) as well as the optimal functioning of **SSRI** medications (Delgado et al., 1994; Wolfersdorf, Maier, Froscher, Laage, & Straub, 1994).

Choose vibrant orange, red, and yellow vegetables and fresh fruits to ensure you get all of the vitamins you need. Healthy fats, such as omega3 oils found in olive oil and fish, have a reputation for assisting the brain's function.

After that, get some rest! Not only does your brain need 8 hours of sleep a night to relieve stress, but it also requires it to repair and produce new cells. (For more information on this subject, see Andrew Weil's, Daniel Amen's, and Kathleen DesMaisons' work.)

<u>The following suggestions will assist you in increasing your nutrient intake:</u>

- ✓ Include protein, which aids in the production of neurotransmitters in the brain.
- ✓ Include dark green, leafy vegetables, which aid in the formation of new brain cells.

- ✓ To ensure that you have all of the trace elements you need, take a multivitamin.
- ✓ Eat daily meals so that you have access to nutrients consistently.
- ✓ Make sure you're getting enough good fats and avoiding hydrogenated oils.
- ✓ Get enough sleep so the body can use nutrients for cell growth and repair.

It's not always easy to take control of the things that make your body anxious, but it's still worthwhile. Physical arousal can be reduced by exerting mental effort and altering your physical environment, both inside your body and outside in the world.

Technique 2: Breath

"Breath," says Faith Hill. Inhale." Breathing is the most powerful method for controlling the nervous body. The power of breath regulation to relax your physiology is almost magical. Breathing has the advantage of working even though you don't think it would. You already know how to breathe, so when you learn to apply breathing to anxiety, you won't be starting from scratch. If you learn how to use breathing and remember to use it, no matter what physical arousal symptoms you are experiencing, you can feel more relaxed right away. Breathing techniques can help with a variety of anxiety issues.

Some breathing methods include:

- ✓ Diaphragmatic breathing to interrupt panic until it begins
- ✓ Breathing to diminish and then avoid panic after it has begun
- ✓ Associating deep breathing with progressive muscle relaxation, so taking a breath will alleviate stress by cueing muscle relaxation
- ✓ Breathing exercises to keep the body relaxed and prevent stress.

PRACTICING DIAPHRAGMATIC

BREATHING

Before you read any more, try this: Take a deep breath in and out slowly. You've just demonstrated the power of diaphragmatic breathing if you've done it. The prefrontal cortex (P.F.C.) of your brain made the executive decision to breathe, and the cortex sent orders to the parts of your brain that will ensure that all of the muscles and organs required to perform a breath are activated. Respiration and heart rate are continuously directed and controlled in your medulla, a primitive part of your brain, without your conscious involvement. You may, however, alter the rate of that respiration by making a conscious decision. It reduces sympathetic arousal and boosts parasympathetic nervous system function, which lowers physical arousal. Your panic symptoms will fade if you keep doing this.

When a panic attack has started, diaphragmatic breathing is the only way to avoid it. Even if you don't believe it will succeed, it's the only thing a person can do as an act of will. The act of breathing has an immediate effect on the human body's physiology. Even before fear sets in, the body's nervous state affects breathing. However, in times of panic, breathing becomes shallow and rapid without warning, and gulps or gasps may occur. Hyperventilation, which induces dizziness, is a result of excessive breathing. The antidote to hyperventilation is diaphragmatic breathing.

As you prepare to begin, pay attention to your breathing. Please make a note of your thoughts, so they don't get lost. Answer the following questions:

- ✓ Is the rate of your inhalation and exhalation consistent?
- ✓ Do you take a breath break now and then? When do you think this will happen?
- ✓ Do you have a feeling of being rushed or out of breath?
- ✓ Is it possible to say if you're breathing into your lungs or just your chest?

Set aside a portion of your concentration the next time you're under duress to notice how your breathing changes when you're stressed. If you're worried about having to talk in a group, keep an eye on your breathing. Take note of how you breathe while you're disagreeing. Take a moment to notice your breathing, even though you're under a lot of pressure. You may be shocked to hear that you haven't been filling your lungs or holding your breath while inhaling.

Make a map to watch your breath. Make a checkmark next to anything that applies, and make a note if you notice something else about your breathing.

Anywhere, can be breathed. If you're tired at work or home, you can relax privately or in public without being noticed. If you practice this rigorously, you can use it immediately for panic attacks. The duration of a panic attack would decrease instantly.

If you decrease the effect of a panic attack effectively for a few weeks, you can see a decline in the level of panic. Stopping panic calms the basal ganglia and allows it to panic less frequently.

<u>Practice first by lying down or standing—then you can breathe anywhere without warning. Be mindful that the goal is not to change how you breathe when you do your everyday work but to change how you breathe when you begin to fear actively.</u>

1. Lie flat on your back or stand with your feet slightly apart and your legs relaxed. It will allow you to feel the movement in your belly, which should expand when you inhale and contract when you exhale.
2. Place your hand on your stomach and rest it there. You'll be able to tell if you're breathing deeply enough and if your chest is tight by doing so.
3. To begin the exercise, fully exhale all of the air in your lungs. Inhale slowly and deeply through your nose. Inhale equally, as though

you would fill your lungs in fair, even quantities from the bottom to the top. Consider how a water balloon fills up when connected to a faucet. The water extends the upper portion first, filling and widening the bottom first. When you inhale, visualize your breath filling a bubble in your belly, becoming heavier and warmer. Finding a rhythm that works for measuring your breathing in and out will allow you to breathe evenly. To aid in getting a measured, even breath, count until you feel exactly full (e.g., a slow 1, 2, 3, 4). To fill your lungs with smooth inhalations, it's likely that you'll take 3 to 6 counts. If you don't like counting, imagine a sentence like "I am slowly filling my lungs with air." "I'm slowly but steadily emptying my lungs." Fill up uniformly, with no gulps or gasps, so that the top of the balloon is reached literally (in your mental picture of the balloon) just in time to release the breath at the same even, measured rate.

4. Slowly exhale until your lungs are hollow, taking longer than you did to inhale. Exhaling slowly and steadily is recommended. Consider blowing at a candle flame to drive it but not to extinguish it. If you don't give your body enough time to swap oxygen and carbon dioxide, you'll get dizzy, which is a symptom you want to avoid, not promote!

5. If you begin to feel dizzy, exhale for two counts longer or pause for two counts at the end of your exhalation before inhaling again.

6. Put in some effort! To calm down a panic attack, practice diaphragmatic breathing. If they've practiced their panic management techniques, most people who panic forget about them right away. You must practice diaphragmatic breathing whether or not you are experiencing fear.

❖ **Make "Breathing Minutes" a habit.**

Try this "breathing minutes" exercise 10 or more times a day for 30 days. When you're waiting for something, practice diaphragmatic breathing for a minute at a time. You don't have to be standing or sitting down to do this. You can do it whenever you want:

- you sit at a stoplight
- You're on the phone
- You wait in a store inline
- During a T.V. broadcast, you see the advertisements
- You wait to heat some food with the microwave
- You expect a friend at school or work
- You're expecting someone to pick up in the car
- You want the machine to boot
- The instructor will receive the examination papers.
- You wait for an immediate post or a telephone or text message
- You expect a meeting to begin

Choose one time of day after you've practiced for seven days when you know you'll have a few minutes to yourself. Early morning, late evening or lunch break are the perfect times for most people. One minute of breathing will be added to this one continuous time per day. You'll do the 1-to 2-minute practices 7 to 9 times a day for the next 7days, but you'll add 1 minute to the time you chose when you can be uninterrupted per day. You should be able to practice for 7 to 8 minutes every day by the end of the week. Once you can hold your breath for this long, you've set the stage for breathing for other critical purposes like deep relaxation, meditation, and cueing the stress response to turn off. You will finally avoid practicing as you become more adept at using diaphragmatic breathing automatically when panic symptoms arise. If you suffer from the stiffness and tightness that comes with being "uptight" or "wired," you can use daily breathing to cause muscle relaxation. You may generate a cue for relaxation by deliberately observing how your muscles relax when you breathe. Later, when you consciously breathe in that steady, profound manner, your muscles will release the tension that has built up.

People will still face challenges before they can make diaphragmatic breathing work for them. However, practice is needed to make it a habit. Among the most popular roadblocks are:

When fear hits, it is failing to practice or forgetting to breathe. It is why, during the day, I recommend connecting breathing to a variety of times, locations, and activities. It would be easier to recall if you do the following:

- Imagine yourself breathing in a sink, a car, a machine, on the phone, or in front of the television. It will serve as a cue to go there and train.
- Keep track of everything. Some people are better at remembering things if they write them down. You should carry an index card with you

at all times and write down what you practice. The repetition of noticing when you practice will solidify it in your mind and make it easier to recall the next practice.

- Take a note to remember to relax. When anxiety hits, it's easy to forget to breathe, but the best way is to practice regularly during the day, so keep a reminder in a visible place. When you start to feel nervous, write the word "breathe" on a notecard and pull it out of your pocket or purse.

As fear arises from breathing when breathing deeply, some people become nervous. Some people are afraid of losing their breath, and they are worried about panicking while learning something new. Others find the act of breathing to be a trigger for their anxiety. Since incorrect methodology and giving in to anxious thoughts are the most common causes, you'll need two types of assistance. Work with someone who can observe and correct the breathing technique. If that doesn't work, you'll want to see if trauma or another, more profound source of fear makes it difficult for you to do breathing exercises without feeling anxious.

When breathing does not appear to be effective, it's infrequent for diaphragmatic breathing not to affect anxiety reduction. Keep an eye on how you're practicing. You may be filling your chest while keeping your abdomen close or that you're holding your breath for a portion of your breathing. I once had a debate with two graduate students in my class who kept on sucking their stomachs in a while inhaling. They've been doing the exact opposite of what their bodies should have done in a normal situation, but they've been breathing wrongly for so long that they've kept doing it. When they learned to let their abdomen expand while inhaling, they were astounded by how strange it felt. It can be beneficial to have others watch you breathe because it can be challenging to notice what you're doing yourself.

When you're having trouble focusing. When practicing breathing, everyone's mind wanders with intrusive thoughts. <u>**It is very true if you add a moment to at least one of your daily breathing exercises. The most effective way to deal with distractions is to:**</u>

- When you realize you've been distracted, think to yourself, "Oh. A thought." Simply note, without passing judgment on yourself for being distracted. Do not get irritated with yourself or with your breathing. Consider your reflections as passing clouds in the sky. You don't need to avoid them, investigate them, or be annoyed by their presence.
- Bring your focus back to your breathing.
- Concentrate on breathing's physical sensations, such as expanding your lungs, waistband against your belly, or moving your back against a chair. When your breath passes through your nostrils or out your mouth, notice how it moves.
- Count to keep track of your speed and to keep your attention on your breathing.

When inhaling becomes difficult. You may feel constricted or obstructed as if there is a blockage in your airflow, or you may be unable to fill your lungs. When you're nervous, you'll do something like this. To begin, make sure you're standing up straight and loosen any constrictive clothing you're wearing, such as tight jeans or neckties. If the issue isn't as clear, the cause may be mental, and it's best to practice breathing in therapy and explore the emotional reactions to the breath. **<u>Consider the following questions:</u>**

- ✓ What is the location of the constraint or obstruction?
- ✓ How does it make you feel? Is there an expression or term to explain it?
- ✓ What does it seem to be? What is the form, color, and size of it?

<u>After that, you should:</u>

- ✓ Make a simple mental image of the block.
- ✓ Guide your breath to the block's heart.

✓ Focus on what happens when you relax. When you become aware of emotional obstructions or limits, as long as you do not try to drive them away, they will permanently vanish.

✓ Consider what it would take to make the block smaller or disappear, and then picture yourself doing so.

When you're dealing with physical disabilities, asthma, or other lung conditions, make it impossible for some people to breathe. If that's the case, you'll need to contact your pulmonary specialist to find a faster breathing rate, shorter duration, and minor discomfort. For those with chronic lung disease or pulmonary issues, lowering the speed and length of breath is typically the key to make diaphragmatic breathing useful.

A Final Thought on Diaphragmatic Breathing When you practice, you will become more aware of your breathing. This technique is easy to learn but challenging to master. To effectively relieve tension by breathing, you must first remember to do so! You can forget to breathe if you are anxious or stressed before it becomes a habit. This process takes some time to become smooth and straightforward. Efficient breathing takes time and effort before it becomes second nature. "After a while, it's automatic!" as the commercials used to say about operating a V.W. Beetle stick shift.

❖ Breathing for Minimal Arousal

When people are placed in awkward positions, they tense up and try not to show it. They appear to remain motionless, their breathing slow and their bodies tense. In other words, they build up a lot of muscle tension and set a hair-trigger on their fear, anticipating flushing, sweating, trembling, and quivering as soon as they think someone is looking at them. They could also have a panic attack if they begin to believe that they would be unable to handle the situation. With that level of anxiety, it's essential to take precautions, such as breathing deeply and assisting yourself in remaining stable as you plan to do what you fear. You're less likely to focus on your fears if you concentrate on your breathing, and your parasympathetic nervous system will help you prevent excessive physical arousal if you're breathing. The less worried you are, the less likely you are to suffer from anxiety symptoms.

For example, you could be in a business meeting where you're supposed to offer a report on your activities, and you don't like how you feel when everyone is staring at you. As you wait to talk, take a few deep breaths to keep from being nervous. Perhaps you're preparing to do something you've never done before, such as try out for a sports team, give a speech, or speak up to your boss about an issue. In such cases, you may use preventive diaphragm ventilation. Even when confronted with difficult circumstances, you will remain physically calm.

The "In 2, Out 2-4-6-8- 10" method of calming breathing is an incredibly useful 1-minute breathing

<u>exercise when you only have a limited period and
need to be subtle. It is how it goes:</u>

1. Take a two-count inhale.
2. Take a two-count exhalation.
3. To the count of two, take a deep breath. Take a deep breath to the count of two.
4. Exhale four times.
5. Take two deep breaths.
6. Take a deep breath and exhale to the count of six.
7. Take two deep breaths.
8. Take a deep breath out to the count of eight.
9. Take two deep breaths.
10. Exhale to a count of ten.

You might also be in hectic or emotionally difficult circumstances from which you need a break but can only be left for a short while. The "5-Count Energizing Air" is a good breathing technique, but it's challenging to use subtly. If you can leave the room or use the toilet, this is a good idea<u>. *In reality, if you're washing your hands, it's a good idea to use this breathing*</u>

1. Inhale slowly to a count of five(5).
2. Huff your breath out in short bursts to the count of 5: huh-huh-huh-huh-huh-hun.

You will reenter the high-stimulation world with less anxiety but also with the energy to cope after taking a few minutes out and breathing off the nervous energy you've gained. You'll be less likely to get overly concerned about the situation, and your mind will be easier to adapt to whatever occurs.

Breathing is simple to learn but difficult to remember when you're panicked, tense, or afraid of what's about to happen. Since fear tends to make you forget what you're supposed to do, practice breathing until it comes naturally. Breathing exercises remain useful well after you've mastered anxiety management, as they serve as a foundation for meditation, relaxation, and other constructive approaches to coping with life's usual stresses.

Technique 3: Practice Mindfulness With Shifting Awareness

While mindfulness does not seem to have anything to do with anxiety management, it is a powerful way to acknowledge the existence of painful physical stimuli without being alarmed and move the focus of consciousness away.

As an anxiety management technique, mindfulness is a state of consciousness that can be achieved in several ways and has many benefits and applications. Psychotherapists are finally paying attention to mindfulness in study and practice (Kabatt-Zinn, 2005; Siegel, 2007). It's a way of being completely present in the present moment. Anxiety is the antithesis of such presence. Worrying about what was or would be is inherent in anxiety. It rarely focuses on the present moment. You are not worried if anything negative is happening right now. You're probably struggling with it right now. Of course, something happening right now could frighten you, but you're still dealing with it, not thinking about it.

Those who have studied its effects on the brain and body have shown carefulness to calm the brain.

Mindfulness reduces the physical effects of stress by helping people to be more concentrated, more likely to find solutions to problems, and more able to stay calm in the face of everyday life's stresses (Benson, 1996; Kabat- Zinn, 2005; J. Schwartz et al., 2005; Siegel, 2007; Williams, Teasdale, Segal, & Kabat-Zinn, 2007).

To enjoy the full benefits of awareness, you must be disciplined and practice different techniques to learn this advantageous meditation technique and live in the world. Thich Nhat Hanh (1999), Kabat-Zinn (2005), Benson (1996), and Siegel (2007), among others, have written books that will help you understand what mindfulness is and how to practice it. However, only one aspect of mindfulness is addressed in this chapter: shifting consciousness.

Even if you're not committed to making a lifestyle change, there's a careful technique that can help those concerned about what's happening to their bodies. This exercise will help you distinguish between what is actual and what is imagined over time and help you disregard transient and insignificant bodily sensations.

What Mindfulness with Shifting Awareness Can Do for You?

My customer Sara, who experienced weakening panic in adulthood, began mastering breathing exercises that reduced her fear of death while undergoing panic attacks. She, on the other hand, created a new problem. She started to worry that she'd still be scared. "After all," she explained, "this panic had complete power over me, and I had always been so strong." Sara was overly concerned with any minor bodily sensation, assuming that each tingle signaled the start of a panic attack. She was essentially instilling fear in herself due to minor, everyday changes in her physical condition. All it took was a slight chill or a fleeting flutter in her stomach for her to start hyperventilating in fear that panic was approaching, which, of course, it would be with her mind focused on the sensation.

She had to learn to turn her attention away from her physical condition and then to the other aspects of her life. She needed to learn to pay attention to the outside world rather than her own. Keep in mind that our minds collect input from all of our senses while the hypothalamus monitors our organs and bloodstream information.

Learning to guide concentration and attention are critical aspects of mindfulness, as is paying attention to the outside world.

You gain control of how you experience life by focusing your attention on what's happening around you. You're the one that decides what you'll do with your time. Your ability to analyze yourself improves as well. Self-observation is necessary to use the brain to observe your thoughts and emotions. The ability to use the brain to manipulate the brain, which is unique to humans, is at the core of anxiety management, and it is most visible when deciding what to focus on. When physical stimuli are bothering you and concentrating on them, serve no useful purpose; shifting your attention away from observing the outside world will help you relax. Self-soothing is a valuable life skill.

Mindfulness combined with changing consciousness can help to de-emphasize physical stimuli and effectively divert attention away from them. Panic attack victims are acutely conscious of their physical sensations and changes.

People who experience flushing, sweating, or trembling due to the fear of being judged by others are acutely conscious of their feelings.

When a person concentrates on these stimuli, they are doomed to have the physical reaction they are most afraid of. This method, which teaches you how to regulate your awareness, will help you avoid concentrating your mind on feelings right away, preventing the symptoms you're afraid of developing. You'll learn to move from being conscious of your inner feelings to be aware of your surroundings.

Practicing Mindfulness with Shifting Awareness

It's best to try this approach with a buddy who will guide you through the exercise while focusing on your comprehension and not splitting your attention by reading the instructions.

1. <u>Have your partner read these steps aloud:</u>
   - Take note of the air's coolness.
   - Take note of the airflow pressure.
   - Take note of how the movement feels in your nose, throat, trachea, and lungs.
   - Pay attention to how your body moves against your clothes and the chair you're sitting in.
   - Exhale through your nose or mouth, following your breath out of your body.
   - Take note of how humid the air is.

- Note how airflow pressure is reversed as it passes through your throat, sinuses, nose, and mouth.
- Consider how air passes through your lungs, trachea, throat, and nose or mouth.
- Pay attention to how your body reacts to your clothing and the chair you're sitting in.

2. **<u>Without opening your eyes, exhale and become aware of your surroundings.</u>**
   - Pay attention to any sound in your world, paying particular attention to its location and intensity.
   - Increase your sensitivity to the smells around you.
   - If you're in a place with other people around, turn your attention to world movement.

3. Return your attention to your body and exhale once more.
   - Be aware of the air's coolness.
   - Pay attention to the air pressure.

- Pay attention to the movement of your nose, mouth, trachea, and lungs.
- Take note of how your body shifts with your clothing and the chair you're sitting in.
- Add this to your awareness: Pay attention to your heartbeat.
- Remember how warm the air feels when you exhale.
- Feel the airflow sensation reversed as it passes through your throat, sinuses, nose, and mouth.
- Pay attention to how air flows into your lungs, trachea, throat, nose, and mouth.
- Focus on how your body feels as it pushes against your dress and your sitting seat.

4. <u>**Exhale your consciousness into the room while keeping your eyes closed.**</u>
   - Pay attention to any sound in the world, paying close attention to its location and intensity.
   - Increase your sensitivity to the smells in the world.

- If you're in an environment with other people around, turn your attention to world movement.

5. <u>**When you inhale, return your attention to your body.**</u>

  - Be aware of the air's coolness.
  - Pay attention to the air pressure.
  - Pay attention to how your nose, throat, trachea, and lungs react to movement.
  - Take note of how your body shifts concerning your clothing and the chair you're sitting in.
  - Note the rhythm of the heart.
  - Increase your consciousness by noticing the flow of blood or energy into your body or limbs.
  - Pay attention to the air's warmth.
  - Feel the airflow sensation reversed as it passes through your throat, sinuses, nose, and mouth.
  - Pay attention to how air flows into your lungs, trachea, throat, nose, and mouth.

- Consider how your body feels when it rubs against your clothing and the seat you're in.

6. <u>When you exhale, turn your focus to the outside world once more.</u>
   - Pay attention to any sound in the world, paying close attention to its location and intensity.
   - Pay attention to the smells of your surroundings.
   - If you're in an environment with other people around, turn your attention to world movement.

7. <u>Begin by being aware of light passing through your eyelids, and then gradually open your eyes, taking in the color of the light and then the objects you can see with your vision as you become completely conscious and aware of the situation.</u>

Mindfulness and Panic Attacks

By mastering this mindfulness technique, you will avoid being afraid of physical stimuli that cause you to think about whether or not you're about to have an anxiety attack. People manage their fear by avoiding circumstances where they have panicked previously. When they attempt to reenter such cases, they often state that they are watching for fear to return. These people are often afraid of what would happen if they ignore their panicked feelings. They genuinely ask, "How can I do this?" It might seem amusing, but it is not. What if I get so worked up that I don't see it coming?" "Did you ever have and do not know about a panic attack?" I always react.

If you don't have enough breathing or mindfulness experience to prevent a panic attack from developing, the attack will most likely occur. The strategies to monitor the thoughts that accompany this will be discussed in the next segment, Part III. However, adopting the attitude of "don't be afraid of fear" is a brilliant idea. What you need to do now is devise a strategy for dealing with a panic attack. If you need a reminder, write down this schedule and keep it with you. Solutions for conditions such as driving, being in a public location, and so on must be identified. Then, before approaching the situation for the first few occasions, you should check the written choices. Getting a strategy gives you hope, which can help you feel less anxious. Staying put and breathing before the panic subsides is always the best choice.

Driving is a little different in that you want to make sure you don't hurt someone else, so pull over and take a few deep breaths before your anxiety passes.

This fantastic, easy technique had a significant impact on one of my clients. When she returned to driving on the highway, diverting her attention to the outside world was incredibly beneficial. She did some diaphragmatic breathing and redirected her focus back to the road and the acts of driving the car as she began to experience feelings that might be a harbinger of a panic attack.

Even though her strategy allowed her to stop if her symptoms worsened, focusing her mind on the road was enough to keep her from having a full-fledged panic attack. She regained trust in her ability to drive without fear after just a few trips on the road without panicking.

Mindfulness and Flushing, Sweating, Or Embarrassed Anxiety

As previously mentioned, avoiding the discomfort that others will notice—slight signs of flushing, sweating, or shaking—is an essential part of reducing nervousness attacks. The peripheral nervous system causes these symptoms, and once they've started, they're more difficult to stop panic itself, partly because others are aware of them. Finally, once you stop worrying whether you flush or not, you'll reduce the propensity to do so. However, the best way to avoid these symptoms is to learn how to remain calm in conditions that might

trigger anxiety. Depending on which path is most helpful at the time, mindfulness with shifting awareness will lead you inward or outward. Shy people can prevent the overstimulation that can cause blushing, sweating, or flushing if they are flustered by focusing on their inner breathing rather than the ambient commotion.

It is a fantastic technique for pulling the mind away from anxiety or fear and turning your focus to the present moment. You can achieve mindfulness with shifting consciousness in any environment without being obvious—as long as you keep your eyes downcast and not closed. Being in the present, not in the future or past, is the antithesis of anxiety, as I said before. The strategy itself doesn't change depending on whether you're nervous, anxious, or panicked—you can use it in all of these situations—but the pacing can. Since worry and panic can strike at any time and for any reason, this "do it anywhere" strategy is ideal for people who worry.

Technique 4: Relax

For controlling the nervous body, relaxation has a wide range of applications. It can be used to remain calm in stressful situations, change gears at the end of a long day, calm the mind, increase thinking clarity, alleviate stress on the body, and more. Relaxation, Technique #4, provides several options for dealing with various types of stress and anxiety.

Stressed people are often described as "uptight." The majority of people tighten up physically when they are stressed. They don't realize they're tense until their backs are knotted, or their heads hurt. Anxiety sufferers struggle with physical relaxation. People with high arousal and nervous anxiety aren't aware of how hard their necks and shoulders, lower backs, buttocks, and legs have contracted until they experience pain. Tight muscles cause tension headaches in the head and neck that block blood flow or interfere with nerve function.

<u>Mental tension also causes physical tension. As an illustration:</u>

- People prone to fear are more likely to expect trouble, causing them to become tense.

- People who suffer from social anxiety are afraid of being embarrassed, which causes them to become worried when going out in public.

- People who suffer from generalized anxiety are in a constant state of mental exhaustion. Tightness is also generated as a result of this. Too much norepinephrine (N.E.) in the pons induces vigilance and amplifies the "wired" sensation in the basal ganglia, resulting in physical stress. Muscle relaxation can be beneficial to everyone, but people with generalized anxiety are more likely to need to do it regularly. They deal with the mental stress of the ruminating anterior cingulate gyrus, which causes muscles to tighten and tighten over time, in addition to the tension of vigilance and high drive. Worriers should learn to cue relaxation regularly to overcome the anxiety that builds up during the day. Before entering a public environment that they are afraid of, people with social anxiety need to calm their bodies.

Tense-And-Release Progressive Muscle Relaxation

Progressive muscle stimulation for pain relief is a "first-line" treatment for the nervous body's physical tension. It works to relieve the symptoms and illnesses associated with chronic tightness in the neck, back, jaw, and other body areas.

The parasympathetic nervous system slows cardiac rates and respiration and lowers blood pressure by intentionally relaxing muscles with slow, deep breathing. It not only relieves tension-related stiffness and aches but also reduces arousal levels, making it more difficult for physical nervous symptoms to manifest. Deep relaxation can be learned by methods like yoga or meditation and specific martial arts, although these methods require advanced instruction from a practitioner of those arts. The method of progressive muscle relaxation described here is simple to understand and is the best solution for people who suffer from generalized anxiety.

This technique's primary purpose is to relax all of your muscles in a systematic manner. It'll take 10-15 minutes to complete. This method's instructions can be found in the following script. Feel free to add reminders to feel warm as the muscles release to the directions. You can include images if you want. People who are rational and pragmatic perform better without imagery, but you can add imagery to steps 3 and 5 to improve this technique. When it comes to children, using imagery is particularly useful. If you're leading relaxation, make sure the imagery you're using is comforting to the other individual before you get started.

1. Ensure that you are lying flat or sitting with your neck straight in a comfortable posture.
2. Close your eyes and think about something. Concentrate entirely on each muscle group's sensations.

3. Incorporate a visual element into the procedure. Consider how the sun is steadily shining on you as you go through this workout, starting with your toes and going up your body. (Other photos that perform well include ice cream melting, Jello, or butter softening in the sun.)

4. If you're sitting up, start at the top and work your way down. If you're lying down, start at your feet and work your way up, one muscle group at a time.

   - Tense the muscle group, keep it, then relax it. Tense the toes, for example, by curling them tighter and tighter. Now is the time for you to go.

   - Allow yourself to be enveloped by the warmth. Feel the warmth and energy flowing through your muscles.

   Feel the warmth spread through your toes with each exhalation of air.

- Tension, catch and release three times more. (After only one or two tightenings, it's surprising how much stress remains.)

5. When you relieve each muscle group's tension, feel the warmth and vitality that fills the muscles. If you're using a particular picture, such as the sun touching each part of your body, Remember the picture as you go through each group.

6. Muscle groups can be numbered in the following order:

   - To tighten the scalp, lift the brows.
   - Lift the brows on the forehead.
   - Tighten your face by squinting your eyes, wrinkling your nose, and pursed lips.
   - Neck circles are bad for the spine, so avoid them.

<u>Instead, consider the following:</u>

Allow your head to drop forward, pulling your chin toward your chest as you do so. If you're very close, you'll feel the stretch down to your lower back.

Before leaning back in the opposite direction, bring your head to a fully upright position.

You'll feel the stretch as far down as your shoulder blade if you tilt your head to one side with the ear going straight toward the shoulder. Feel the warmth flow in where the stretching was when your head is upright.

- Shoulders—hunch up your shoulders and then relax.
- By clenching your palm, you can tighten your forearm, wrist, and side.
- Back and abdomen—imagine a cord pulling your belly button (navel) toward your spine, then slowly release it.
- Squeeze the buttocks together to tighten.

- Thighs—tighten the quad muscles by tensing and relaxing them.

- Tighten your calves and shins by pointing your toes and feeling the stretch down your shin and calf contraction. Then, raising the toe and bringing the heel down, do the same. Feel the calf extension and the shin contraction.

- •Curl your toes or press your foot into the ground to tighten your feet and toes.

7. If you started at the top and worked your way down, you should have a good understanding of how the soles of your feet feel connected to the earth through the surface. If you started from the bottom up, you should feel relaxed from head to toe.

8. Take note of how completely comfortable, warm, and at ease you are. Allow yourself to stay comfortable for as long as you like. If you're moving on to another task, allow

yourself to stay physically relaxed while still refreshed, alert, and completely present.

Muscle Relaxation with Children and Elderly Adults

There is no reason why older adults cannot use this method because it can be performed sitting or lying down. A keynote, as with all workouts, is never to do something that causes pain. It's not unexpected to feel a little sore in the wake of loosening up tense muscles. However, it's more similar to "great touchiness" than torment. Make sure you or the people you're teaching are aware of the difference.

If you're using this strategy with kids, turn stretching and soothing muscle groups into a game to keep their attention. While children rarely experience muscle soreness due to stress, learning to relax is an essential part of developing healthy habits. Using pictures of animals that younger children may relate to, such as a sun-drenched cat or a lion yawning. Using the "stretch and release" language rather than "tense and release" works well for these pictures. Stretching as a group activity in the classroom will help children and adolescents relax before challenging activities such as taking an exam.

Sphere of Light Imagery for Relaxation

As I previously stated, many people find that imagery for muscle relaxation is beneficial. Slowing respiration and heart rate, opening capillaries, and causing parasympathetic relaxation are all advantages.

<u>There are several different relaxation images, but the "sphere of light" is beneficial.</u>

1. Visualize a bubble of light and energy hovering over your head.
2. The color light is the one you think of when you think of harmony, calm, healing, or electricity. You can draw yourself as much as you want because it's abundant and can't be drained.

3. Breathe this lovely, humid, vivid, colorful energy through the top of your head as you inhale.

4. Feel the surge of energy that flows through your scalp when you exhale.

5. Breathe energy and light into each of your body parts (face, head, neck, shoulders, arms, hands, fingers, torso, hips, buttocks, thighs, knees, shins, calves, ankles, feet, and toes), and feel the energy flow into those muscles as you exhale.

6. Feel the flow of the beautiful, soft, vivid, colorful energy through each body part.

7. Visualize energy flowing through your spine and out the other side, as if you were planting roots in the ground.

8. Visualize energy flowing through the soles of your feet and through the earth, which can absorb any amount of energy and transform it into life energy.

9. Allow the energy that is emitted from your pores to surround your body.

10. Think of a word or sound associated with total relaxation, such as "calm" or "peace," or "ah" or "mmm."

11. For the rest of the day, this energy acts as a barrier to negativity, preventing any criticism, rejection, harsh words, or ill-treatment from entering your heart. The barrier is permeable to all positive energies, allowing encouragement, acceptance, and love to reach the heart immediately.

12. As the energy envelope disappears during the day, take a deep breath, imagine the energy and light, and say or hear the soothing sound or word you want to refresh it.

One-Breath Muscle—Or "Cued"—Relaxation

Diaphragmatic breathing happens almost naturally when performing muscle relaxation techniques. It's natural to breathe evenly while letting go of the stress in each muscle group. When you practice muscle relaxing, start noticing how the body feels. When you finish a relaxation, you'll probably find that your breath is even and deep, and your muscles are relaxed as well.

Muscle relaxation is a way of dealing with physical tension that can be used for the rest of one's life. Physical tension does not go away with one session of relaxation because it can be caused by activity in the basal ganglia or an excess of norepinephrine. It will reappear regularly and not always as a result of overt stress. Muscle relaxation, which must be understood and then incorporated into an ongoing symptom-control strategy, is the only way to interrupt the stress caused by basal ganglia activity. In people with nervous bodies, relaxing the muscles decreases the high level of anxiety and the associated pain.

People who suffer from social anxiety or panic will benefit from "one breath" or "cued" relaxation. People who need to remain calm in circumstances where they have previously panicked or in social environments where blushing and sweating are embarrassing may use cued relaxation as a way to keep their bodies calm before approaching a stressful situation.

You can combine diaphragmatic breathing and progressive muscle relaxation to produce cued relaxation once you've mastered both. The combination of breathing and muscle relaxation has several benefits:

• Breathing encourages the parasympathetic nervous system, which calms the organs, and the neuroendocrine system is stimulated during stress. Sympathetic nervous system arousal is quickly triggered in people who have elevated norepinephrine levels, which leads to increased physical and emotional tension. The ability to regulate the body using the brain (the prefrontal cortex decision-making function) is best shown by the decision to breathe. Breathing with muscle relaxation can help interrupt or diminish the stress response in people with overactive stress-response systems, such as those with social anxiety or those who have been traumatized.

- By combining breathing and deep muscle relaxation, one or two complete diaphragmatic breaths may be associated with total relaxation.

Once that link is established, a person can use a regulated deep breath to cue relaxation at any time or in any location.

It's reasonably easy to extend your diaphragmatic breathing and muscle relaxation experience into a cued relaxation once you've experienced it:

1. Take a slow, diaphragmatic breath several times a day to promote the physical release, remembering how you feel when you are deeply relaxed.

2. When you exhale, send harmful energy out of your body and allow relief to flow in behind it across your whole body, using an image that reflects letting go of tension, such as plugging your feet into the earth. Another right image is to send roots from your feet into the ground to bring peace in and release tension into the air.

3. Say something soothing to yourself as you take a long, deep breath in, like, "Now I am breathing in all that is peaceful." I'm exhaling all that isn't peaceful right now." Draw casual comfort inward when inhaling and exhaling the harmful energy, whether using an image or an expression.

4. Exhale and send the energy off in the direction you've pictured. Take note of how your muscles are releasing tension from your head to your fingertips. Rep this exercise several times a day to relieve muscle tension that builds up due to everyday stress and an anxious body's extra tension.

You'll be able to take one breath and feel all of your muscles relax as you get more familiar with this pairing. You can now cue muscle relaxation on command, anywhere and at any moment, without anyone noticing the shift from tight to relaxed.

Exercise to Relax

In people with high levels of stress, physical discomfort, muscle soreness, headaches, digestive distress, and other symptoms of an anxious body are especially noticeable.

Worriers experience tightness all over their bodies as a physical result of their anxiety. You are more likely to take unpleasant situations seriously if you are a "worry wart." Worriers not only experience more stress regularly, but they also cause more stress. Continuous stress can cause physical tension, elevated blood pressure, or problems in almost every body system (Hafen, Karren, Frandsen, & Smith, 1996). These problems are exacerbated in people who worry excessively. Exercising will help you get rid of the adverse effects of stress and anxiety.

The Circular Nature of Pain and Stress

People may become ill, and in pain when stressed, which exacerbates any anxiety, they may be experiencing. It is a dilemma that keeps repeating itself. Increased tension, for example, may exacerbate irritable bowel syndrome (I.B.S.), which then exacerbates tension by making people fearful of the pain of stomach cramps and the interruption of their activities. These diseases may be less severe or occur less often if you learn to relax and relieve stress. People may become ill and in pain when stressed, which exacerbates any anxiety, they may be

experiencing. It is a dilemma that keeps repeating itself. Increased tension, for example, may exacerbate irritable bowel syndrome (I.B.S.), which then exacerbates tension by making people fearful of the pain of stomach cramps and the interruption of their activities. These diseases may be less severe or occur less often if you learn to relax and relieve stress.

Exercise Is a Prime Stress Reliever

According to a large body of study, exercise is beneficial to the mind and body in many ways. Relaxation is supported by exercise. Physical movements provide better physical stimulation than sitting still for the high-energy person with a stressed, nervous body. Aerobic exercise is the most beneficial kind of workout. During periods of high stress, physical exercise helps to flush the body of toxic cortisol by using the adrenaline released during the stress response. It also assists the body in avoiding weight gain due to chronic stress (Talbott, 2002). Finally, since the muscles used are stretched and relaxed afterward, physical exercise encourages relaxation.

Exercising has almost no drawbacks.

Many facets of mental well-being are supported by exercise. It is equally relevant for children and older adults (Bartholomew, 2005; Bremner, 2005; Dunn, 2005). (Larson, 2006; Nelson et al., 2007). It creates a feeling of self-efficacy, which encourages people to control their lives in other ways (Craft, 2005).

Physical activity is essential for overall well-being. Its importance is so great that it should be considered a significant intervention for reducing stress on the brain and body.

Exercise improves blood flow to the brain, linked to many aspects of brain well-being and neurotransmitter levels and overall brain activity. Increasingly, therapists realize that exercise is just as necessary as medication in the recovery of mental illness.

A variety of other steps (Bartholomew, 2005; Cynkar, 2007; Penedo & Dahn, 2005). It could have a more beneficial effect on serotonin levels in people who already have serotonin issues, as shown by studies with depressed people (Kiive, Maaroos, Shlik, Toru, & Harro, 2004). Given that about half of those who suffer from anxiety still have depression, it's reasonable to assume that whatever helps with depression will also help with anxiety.

Anxiety has been shown to respond positively to guidelines similar to those for general physical health (Lancer, 2005; Manager & Motta, 2005). "To support and preserve fitness, the ACSM/AHA [American College of Sports Medicine/American Heart Association][American Sports Medicine/American Heart Association] [American Sports

Medicine/American Heart Association] [American Sports Medicine/American Heart Association] [U.S. Heart Association] [U.S. Heart Association] [U.S. Heart Association] [U.S. Heart Association]

"All healthy adults aged 18 to 65 require moderate aerobic physical activity for at least 30 minutes five days a week or aerobic physical activity for at least 20 minutes three days a week," according to the American Heart Association [writing group.

According to another A.C.S.M. and A.H.A. survey, fewer than half of American adults meet minimum physical activity guidelines for heart health (Haskell et al., 2007). Of course, overexercising can be just as harmful as underexercising (Talbott, 2002). Try the following amount of exercise to get the best anxiety-relieving effect: 5-7 days a week, 25-45 minutes at 70% of your maximum heart rate, a pace that makes contact challenging but not exhausting (Amen, 2000; Sobel & Ornstein, 1996b).

Exercise: Getting Started The most challenging part for people who haven't been exercising regularly is getting underway. Begin by learning about the importance of the physical activity. Remember that the brain's anterior cingulate gyrus (A.C.G.) and orbitofrontal cortex (OFC), which are active in coming up with new solutions to problems, occasionally struggle with these tasks. The A.C.G. might get stuck on "I can't," and the OFC might not be able to come up with alternatives. When it comes to connecting motivation to the exercise phase, the brain may fall short. It is why, even in the absence of motivation, setting an intention (the executive decision-makers role, the prefrontal cortex) is vital to starting the exercise process. Take the time to gain a thorough understanding of this approach and the inspiration to pursue it.

Someone who does not exercise, taking the dog for a one-block or five-minute extra walk, or getting off the bus sooner, maybe a big step. First, determine which activity will be most effective, and then commit to trying.

<u>Commit to attempting it. The questions and recommendations that follow will assist you in developing an exercise routine.</u>

- Do you enjoy any physical activities? (If the answer is "nothing," consider asking yourself, "What do I recall enjoying?") At first, do not rule out something. Do you recall participating in sports when you were younger? Remember when you were a kid, and you were playing in the yard? Can you recall having a good time riding bikes? Did you dive, or did you play tennis or racket sports?

- Do you have many chances to participate in this activity? And if you can't do exactly what you want, look for anything similar. Perhaps you used to play basketball in high school.

- Is it possible to shoot hoops in a park? Do you have a garden? Are you interested in joining an adult youth team? Consider all of the possibilities. Talking about it in counseling or with a friend or family member will help you develop solutions that would otherwise elude a distracted, nervous person.

- What kind of people would you invite to participate in this activity with you? A workout buddy will help you stay motivated and accountable. If you're starting from the ground up, this can be difficult. The thought that you are not as good as someone else could make you feel embarrassed, particularly if you suffer from social anxiety. Working with a trainer, if you can afford it, is an excellent place to start because they will know how hard you can physically push yourself. However, even deciding to meet a friend at the gym to start and finish simultaneously, or meeting at a nearby track and not necessarily going at the same speed, will motivate you to get started and keep going. Even if you can just commit to taking long walks with your dog, having someone rely on you—a pet or a person!—will motivate you to do so.

- Choose your route! What is the most significant move you can take toward physical activity? Every week, respond to this question until you've completed 25 to 45 minutes of aerobic exercise at 70% of your maximum heart rate. The weekly target should result in small improvements in motivation, as success motivates people to do more.

- Agree to a course of action. It's better if you do it for someone else who can ask you how it went. However, you can make a promise with someone who will follow up with you and see if it was held and what you intend to do next week.

- What would you do if you don't follow through? Using a transparent record-keeping system is one easy way to stay accountable.

- Take stock of your accomplishments and write down your goals for the next week. Short-term stress relief and muscle relaxation are best accomplished by aerobic exercise. It's also beneficial for boosting neurochemical levels in the short term. It encourages healthy brain chemicals over time, and increased blood flow to the brain can improve neurological function.

Stretch to Relax

<u>Staying mentally loose can help with all types of anxiety:</u>

- Staying physically relaxed can help the brain cool down while you're experiencing fear. Panic is less likely to arise as a result of this.
- • The more relaxed people are when they have social anxiety, the less likely their peripheral nervous system is to cause the palpitating heart and flushed face they fear. Physical tranquillity leads to mental tranquillity.
- Loosening tight muscles is particularly beneficial for the worrier.
- Stretching increases blood flow and realigns stressed postures, resulting in increased muscle relaxation.

<u>Stretching for stress relief should be done according to this basic rule:</u> Never, ever, ever, ever, ever, do something hurt, stop right away if it hurts. You can do the stretches anytime. Several of the stretches mentioned below can be done at work, at school, or in any confined space like a car or airplane seat.

Furthermore, they are fast to complete. While thinking about the next question on a test, making a phone call and waiting for the person to respond, or waiting for your machine to perform a task, you can stretch. While one 15-second stretch is appropriate, some stretching experts advise doing multiple 2-second stretches to loosen up. Follow the instincts.

<u>The following is a list of stretches that can be done anywhere:</u>

- Extend your arms. Simply yawn, spread your arms upward, and let out a sigh of relief. Repetition is essential.
- Stretch your back. Try torso relaxation for a gentle backstretch. Try letting your body slide forward with your head gently leading the way

down, bending at the waist, and returning to an upright posture by reversing the motion with your feet comfortably spread apart for support. Consider yourself a puppet being released and then dragged upright by a string.

- Stretch your arms above your head. Once you're straight, try extending the backstretch into an overhead stretch. Raise your hands above your head and slant your head periodically with the help of raising your jawline so your look is straight up. Make this, and it will be gentle.

- Lunges with the legs. When you get up to go for a walk, take a moment to pause and try some gentle leg lunges if you've been sitting for too long or are too tight.

- Stretch your calf muscles. If you can go up or down a few stairs, take a moment to pause and, with your toes placed on the stair's edge, let your heel drop, stretching the back of your neck. Hold for 2 seconds before releasing. It's worth repeating a few times. You should do this one leg at a time while keeping the other foot placed firmly on the stair to avoid losing your balance.

- Head tilt when seated at your desk. You can do a quick head-tilt stretch.

  Do not circle with your neck without taking time off work while talking on the phone, watching TV, or reading. Allow your ear to fall as far as it can without damaging your shoulder. Then lift your head to your full height. Slowly lower your chin to your stomach, feel the stretch in your back, and then lift your head back up. Then lower the other ear toward the opposite shoulder and lift your head once more before allowing your head to feel heavy and slowly fall backward. Check that your head is upright before proceeding to the next stage.

- Arm stretch when seated at your desk. Raise one straight arms overhead, then bend it at the elbow and reach down and toward the other side of your body, as if scratching the other shoulder blade. Then unwind. Reach across your chest with the same arm and wrap your hand around the opposite shoulder. Grab the elbow of the reaching arm with the unoccupied hand and gently apply pressure to increase the shoulder and upper arm stretch.

- The shift in a seated posture. The seated posture adjustment is another way to avoid unconsciously tightening up. If your career needs you to sit for long periods, you can use this preventive measure regularly. It entails rotating through various roles regularly. Place a stool (or merely a box) near your feet to rest them. Sit with one foot elevated for 15 minutes in each spot, then the other, then both, then neither. Place a back pillow or rolled towel behind your lower back, then behind your middle back, and finally behind your upper back. Practicing these stretches will help you stay loose when work or life gets in the way.

Slow Down to Relax

Beginning an exercise regimen can be difficult for certain people. There is hope. Other methods for reducing stress and releasing tension exist. Yoga is also an excellent way to encourage calmness because it helps with body awareness, stress release, breathing, and mindfulness. Heartmath (Childre & Martin, 2000) and neurofeedback (Demos, 2005) are two other approaches you can learn to bring about deep relaxation and stress reduction while also setting the stage for a greater understanding of your emotions. They do, however, involve the guidance of a professional practitioner. For anxiety sufferers who also have chronic pain, biofeedback can be extremely beneficial. It's also a good thing to keep in mind that you don't have to rush or feel rushed. Any tasks that include the leisurely use of time can help to relax the nervous system. <u>An anxious person always wants a</u>

good excuse to do something that seems to be lazy or unproductive, so here are a few good reasons for some relaxing activities:

- Getting a massage is a great way to unwind. Several studies have recorded the therapeutic benefit of massage. Lower stress and anxiety, relax muscles, increase circulation, digestion, excretion, and reduce pain perception have been shown. Emotional triggers oxytocin release, a hormone that promotes calm and relaxation (Field, 2002; Kosfeld, Heinrichs, Zak, Fischbacher & Fehr, 2005). Effleurage, deep-tissue, and relaxation massage are only a few of the many forms of massage available. Even a simple message from a family member will give you a sense of being cared about and help you relax. Field (2002) found that massage alleviated the symptoms of stress in postpartum mothers. After
- their sessions, the massage community, had statistically significant increases in saliva cortisol

levels, and they were the only ones who had lower anxiety scores.

- Use aromatherapy in a warm bath. Warmth relaxes muscles and activates oxytocin. Aromatherapy uses essential oils to benefit from the medicinal properties of the plants from which they are obtained. Essential oils are sometimes used to promote relaxation or to alleviate anxiety and stress symptoms. The oils are highly concentrated compounds distilled from medicinal plants; critical oil's action mechanism unclear, unknown, but they may function by absorbing through the skin or inhaling physiologically active compounds in the air. Lavender, jasmine, ylang-ylang, sandalwood, bergamot, and rose oils are the most commonly used for depression and anxiety.

- Take a walk in the sunshine. Some of these oils have been shown to have muscle-relaxing and sedative effects. U.V. rays should shield our skin from the sun's U.V. rays. Still, our brains need light stimulation to develop healthy circadian rhythms (which promotes sleep) and to avoid depression and anxiety. In the gray weather seasons, thirty minutes of walking outside are enough light stimulation to avoid serotonin loss. The sun's energy will also help you relax your muscles.

- • DEEPLY breathe when spending time near a body of water that is lapping or running—a lake, a river, or the sea. The sounds are relaxing, and the ionization of the air near bodies of water makes it easier to unwind.

Sleep!

It is seriously slowing things down! Good health, including mental health, is based on adequate sleep. When you are tired, it isn't easy to relax. Sleep is harmed when a person has anxiety for various reasons, depending on the cause of the anxiety. It involves a variety of different parts of the brain. When serotonin levels are insufficient, the pineal gland's development of melatonin is also disturbed. Melatonin is a hormone that regulates drowsiness and reawakening and is related to daylight/nightfall. When anxiety disrupts sleep, the body's normal melatonin development rhythm is disrupted. When norepinephrine levels are too high, arousal makes it challenging to fall asleep and, more importantly, to stay asleep. Activities that promote deeper sleep can be reduced by physical arousal. When the basal ganglia contribute to high drive, it can be challenging to relax at night. Pay attention to how you treat evening activities well before bedtime so that the basal ganglia overdrive can be settled with activities that encourage physical and mental calm.

Everyone is affected by stress, but people with anxiety who are also under stress from other causes face a "double whammy" when it comes to sleep. Learning stress management techniques can improve sleep.

There's no other way to gain intense mental relaxation promoting healthy sleep. Also, meditation, which has many health benefits for mental and physical well-being, is not a replacement for sleep. Overwork and attempting to keep up with tasks can trigger restless sleep or short nights, making anything else about getting anxiety more difficult. Here are a few simple ways to improve the consistency of your sleep.

Create a Sleeping Habit When people sleep at regular hours, they find it easier to fall asleep, stay asleep, and wake up refreshed. The pineal gland, melatonin synthesis, and circadian rhythm all play a role in sleep. Anxiety conditions, caffeine intake, overwork, or staying up too late interrupt the nervous body's routines, challenging to reestablish. Regain control of your schedule by going to bed and waking up at the same time every day. It will take some time to work, so don't give up too soon. Except on weekends or days off from work, you cannot sleep more than an hour earlier or later.

Making time for sleep is another part of getting enough of it. Sleeping is considered a sign of weakness in the United States, although most adults need 712 to 8 hours of sleep, teens need 9 to 10 hours, and children need more hours depending on their age. Even if they try, anxious people who sleep for only Ganda31hours can have difficulty embracing this idea or staying asleep. However, there is a real psychological and emotional benefit to sleeping more. According to research, a well-rested person gets as much work done as someone who is up for more extended periods because they are more energetic and effective during the day.

To begin having enough sleep, go to bed early enough that you can stay in bed for a full 8 hours, even though you wake up earlier for a while. Until you can sleep for 8 hours, you should expect to stay in bed and rest while implementing the sleep hygiene techniques (described on the following pages) that will eventually help you sleep. If you've established a daily sleep routine and are sleeping reasonably well, you'll notice that you automatically awaken when you're rested, and you'll learn how much sleep your body requires to feel rested. It's important to note that teenagers have unique circadian rhythms.

Biologically, they may not be able to sleep before midnight (unless exhausted), and they may not be ready to wake up until 9 a.m.

School comes at the worst possible time for the teenage body! Setting time limits on using the internet, phone, or playing video games in the evening to finish homework and school activities in time to sleep is a more significant issue.

For various reasons, including the need to use the bathroom frequently or the inability to produce enough melatonin to sustain sleep cycles, older people can sleep restlessly. Many older adults live in facilities that are either too noisy or too bright. Changing aspects of their climate and lifestyle to make them more sleep-friendly can be beneficial. Before taking medication, try herbal teas like spearmint or chamomile, or a short trial with vitamins like L-tryptophan or melatonin to relax the brain or create melatonin if your health permits (Weill, 1998).

Create a Sleep-Friendly Environment; sleep in a cool, dark bed. These are the ideal conditions for maintaining a healthy circadian rhythm that promotes regular sleep cycles. The amygdala works in the same way it does while you're awake, keeping you alert to threat signals. It reacts to changes in sound, scent, and other factors, causing the brain to wake up. Eliminating the amygdala response requires filtering out external noises (such as talking in another room or noise from the street).

While a room without television or lights is usually preferable, many people claim that they want light or noise (such as television or radio) to drown other noises. However, there are alternatives to watching television for this reason. The amygdala becomes excessively alert when the pitch, sound, and volume of a television shift.

If you have to watch T.V. fall asleep, keep in mind that most televisions have sleep timers. Set the timer and use a white-noise backdrop to drown out outside noises. Prepare the Anxious Brain for Sleep.

Regain control of your schedule by going to bed and waking up at the same time every day.

<u>**Note the following:**</u>

- Avoid watching violent or thrilling television for several hours before going to bed, including late-night news shows! Television features amygdala-stimulating music, startling and sometimes gruesome graphics, and overly enthusiastic voices. Its sole aim is to keep people on the edge of their seats if they miss anything important.

- Take a 20-minute warm bath before going to bed. It relaxes tense muscles and promotes the release of oxytocin, a calming hormone.

- Sleep is when the brain recovers and rebuilds itself from stress and anxiety. It requires a good night's sleep to do this, but it also requires nutrition. By eating well during the day and then enjoying a small high-carbohydrate snack before bed, you can help your brain develop cells.

- •This provides the brain with the requisite insulin and blood sugar levels to use the proteins and nutrients needed to create neurotransmitters while sleeping.

- Herbal teas like catnip or chamomile will help you fall asleep. To get the most out of the plant, steep the tea in boiling water for 5 to 10 minutes.

- Caffeine is a stimulant, so limit it as much as possible, mainly afternoon. If you have trouble sleeping, look over the whole beverage intake—you may not know where caffeine hides or how small quantities can cause problems. Caffeine sensitivity is more common in people living with panic disorder than in the general population.

Make a Plan for How to Get Back to Sleep

Anxiety may trigger disturbed sleep for various reasons, but the inability to fall into deep dream sleep, often called Rapid Eye Movement Sleep, is particularly troubled.

They have what I call "worry dreams," which are anxious nights filled with dreams about everyday issues that seem unsolvable during the night. It is generally advised that disturbing sleepers remain in bed and attempt to return to sleep if they awaken. But when it comes to worrying about dreams, remaining in bed and attempting to return to sleep typically results in the dream continuing in its reflective, never-ending fashion. It's safer to completely awaken for a few minutes and shake off the dream by finishing the subject, dismissing its significance, and then concentrating on something nice while falling back to sleep.

Plan for awake periods if you're a restless sleeper. Pick a subject to think about each night before going to bed. You may wake up with a feeling of foreboding triggered by your brain chemistry rather than something being wrong. It's best to resist the temptation to think about what's wrong, instead directing your attention to the subject you chose for the night and attempting to fall asleep with the pleasant thinking.

Relaxation can be accomplished in various ways, and figuring out which ones work best can take some time. Understanding how anxiety affects you and knowing what forms of distractions and soothing and relaxing techniques work best will help you handle it. It could be the most fruitful time and effort you'll ever put into anxiety management in your life.

MANAGING THE ANXIOUS MIND PART 2

Techniques for treating the nervous body do not need people to assume that they will work; they will if you put them into practice. However, dealing with an anxious mind necessitates a level of willingness and faith. Worry and anxiety are still present in the restless mind. If one wants to master the strategies for managing the anxious mind discussed in this section, they must be willing to put in continuous effort.

Staying motivated often requires believing that the methods can function, and understanding how these techniques can improve the brain helps foster confidence. Psychotherapy is often needed for effective anxiety management. A therapist may provide necessary knowledge about the brain, and counseling is the best place to get guidance on applying the strategies, which significantly increases the required willingness. A therapist is a constant source of motivation, assistance, and guidance in putting the approaches into practice, which encourages achievement and propels an individual forward when progress appears to be stalling. When anxiety is high, it's challenging to apply the strategies and maintain the effort without a competent person.

<u>Anxiety manifests itself in several forms. The restless mind manifests itself in panicked people as follows:</u>

- ✓ Catastrophizing the result of panic
- ✓ Catastrophizing the result of any physical sensation
- ✓ Fearing panic throughout the future

<u>Worriers with generalized anxiety not only suffer from persistent suicidal feelings but also catastrophizing. Worriers also suffer:</u>

- ✓ Rage catastrophization
- ✓ Guilt
- ✓ Perfectionist tendencies
- ✓ Lack of planning capacity
- ✓ Looking for reassurance
- ✓ Fear, even if it isn't justified

Worry affects people with social anxiety in a particular way. They are also concerned about developing symptoms in situations where they previously felt and seemed nervous. Their way of thinking encourages them to stop rather than face fear. They are put into the following:

- ✓ Fearing that others would shun them.
- ✓ Believing that their issues are inevitable.
- ✓ Negative self-talk about incompetence and insecurity, which leads to avoidance conduct. This segment discusses four methods for dealing with common anxiety-related issues.
- ✓ Technique 5, Catastrophizing, addresses the propensity to catastrophize, affecting individuals with panic attacks, generalized anxiety, and social anxiety. Assuming the worst in a situation will exacerbate symptoms.
- ✓ Technique 6, Stop Anxious Thinking, involves gaining cognitive influence over one's thoughts and shaping their course and frequency.

✓ Technique 7, "Contain Your Anxiety," is a worry-management technique.

There are particular techniques for worrying that are more effective than others.

✓ Technique 8, Talk Yourself Into Changing Behavior, addresses the internal mechanism of social anxiety and the extreme avoidance it causes.

Technique 5: Stop Catastrophizing

This approach aims to halt anxiety-inducing thought patterns. When a thought starts with "Oh, no!" (a process is known as "catastrophizing"), the mind perceives the situation as bad or horrific or assumes the worst is about to happen.

Brain activity is unquestionably responsible for catastrophizing. Suppose a person with panic disorder senses a shift in her physical stimuli and instantly fears a panic attack is about to happen ("Oh, no!"). In that case, she is likely to panic, thus "proving" her assumption that panic is about to happen. Panic is one of the strongest emotions that the brain remembers. Overwhelming physical arousal, accompanied by a pounding pulse, shallow, rapid breathing, dizziness, nausea, tingling, and the emotion of fear, is a condition that can be remembered in a moment.

When a situation—for example, the possibility of a mistake—triggers worry, the limbic system's responsive, overactive limbic system goes into "Oh, no!" mode. In response to the thought, "Oh, no!" a surge of adrenaline rushes through the body, causing stomach-churning panic. So, if a man with primary worry symptoms is worried about making a mistake, his "Oh, no!" will quickly escalate to extreme fear, making a mistake sound like an impossible disaster rather than a simple oversight. The brain is active when people experience the classic blushing, sweating, and shaking symptoms of being afraid of how others will respond.

The amygdala could be swollen or excessively responsive to changes in people's faces. It indicates people with social anxiety note subtle changes that others will overlook while communicating. Furthermore, the oversensitive amygdala misinterprets others' negativity. The slightest shift in the face it sees efficiently produces an "Oh, no!" and sets off fear responses that trigger the embarrassed, flushed look. If a socially insecure person assumes that blushing will result in social rejection, he or she will over-analyze a seemingly insignificant social interaction.

In this case, catastrophic thought is accompanied by an unspoken conviction that there is no way out. The effectiveness of technique #5 is dependent on the left prefrontal cortex (P.F.C.) taking charge of catastrophic perceptions of feelings/thoughts/situations while also calming down the rest of the brain activity causing such emotional anguish.

Technique 5 deals with a variety of catastrophizing feelings. There are some ways to stop catastrophizing and start controlling your thoughts.

Learn That A Feeling Is Just A Feeling

If someone suffering from anxiety starts to doubt how they feel, knowing that "a feeling is just a feeling" can be extremely beneficial. It makes no difference if the anxiety causes red splotches all over the neck and chest, heart palpitations, and noticeable sweating, or if the sensation is a pounding heart, unsettled stomach, and dizziness. These extreme anxiety feelings aren't life-threatening. They're nothing more than feelings. Do they make you feel uncomfortable? Without a doubt, Irritable? Without question. Are you a stranger? Absolutely. Is it bothersome? Definitely, but that's what they are.

The assumption that these stimuli cannot be accepted causes more problems than the sensations themselves because it intensifies the sensations and induces helplessness that makes it difficult to control.

Understanding that a racing heart, a sinking stomach, or a flushed face are all merely emotions, it's one of the most critical things anxiety management. Panic Is Annoying, But It Isn't Deadly Put a stop to the panic. Avoid catastrophizing that it's terrible as soon as you start feeling panicked-like sensations. "Panic is unpleasant," you might say, "it's not going to kill you." The use of the message is crucial. You can then use diaphragmatic breathing to help relieve any disturbing feelings you might have. It's crucial and pays attention to the results to come to believe that "feeling is just a feeling." Even a full-blown panic attack will pass, and you will be unharmed. This technique becomes a compelling way of mitigating disturbing emotions. You can avoid the catastrophizing illusion that fear is horrible and perform breathing exercises to control the nervous body.

Dread is a feeling that can happen even though there is nothing wrong. High levels of norepinephrine, which lead to hypervigilance, can often trigger a gut feeling similar to when something is about to go wrong—that dreadful "uh oh" feeling. It is more likely to happen to overly tense people. A queasy stomach may not be an immediate feeling, such as risk, but it sends a signal to the worrier's brain to search for explanations to justify the feelings felt in the worried body; it sends a signal to look out for something. It engages the thinking process, scans recent events like a radar dish to determine what you should be concerned about. A hypervigilant worrier will discover everything.

You will start to ward off the feeling of doom or fear by telling yourself, "A feeling is just a feeling." It doesn't imply that there's a problem."

The intention then becomes to avoid looking and divert your attention away from your surroundings to focus on breathing or mindfulness. I've worked with people who are resistant to the possibility of distracting themselves from their emotions. "But what if something is wrong and I neglect it?" they sometimes inquire. The key is to determine if the feeling came before the need to search for something. If you replied yes, you should effort to divert your attention away from the unpleasant feeling. "But," you could counter, "what if I'm afraid of anything coming up and I ignore it?" The real trouble isn't so mysterious that you have to go hunting for it, in my opinion. Real trouble seldom shows up subtly. We get a letter that spells it out, a message from someone moaning about what we did (or didn't do), or some other powerful indication that we're in trouble. Also, it's not uncommon for us to feel better after adjusting to the necessity of solving the problem. A current problem that is being addressed produces less anxiety than a future problem.

However, I don't want to downplay fear. There are moments when dread serves as a warning sign. Your unconscious mind detects a problem in those situations, and you sense it until your conscious, thinking brain recognizes it. If the issue comes from irrational feelings of fear or the unconscious mind picking up on real trouble, psychotherapy will help you figure it out. On the other hand, people with anxiety are often so preoccupied with the physical "uh oh" sensation that they rarely see warning signs. You will improve your ability to read

your body and not associate fear with other emotions when you learn to recognize all of the various stimuli that accompany emotions. If dread is an actual warning sign, you'll recognize it and won't be confused about whether or not you should be feeling it. If that is resolved, it is fair to say that the dreadful "uh oh" is more akin to a mental short circuit. Stop catastrophizing this emotion by telling yourself, "Dread is just a sensation that can happen even though nothing is wrong." Then, as soon as possible, divert your attention away from these thoughts, as worrying about hypothetical issues never helps anyone.

Embarrassment Is Just a Feeling

It's difficult for social anxiety sufferers to suppress their flushing, shaking, and sweaty feelings while they're out in public. Stop catastrophizing about these signs by disputing what you think will happen and then dismissing the physical sensations. "Notice is not the same as rejection," tell yourself. Actual, common signs of embarrassment—blushing, sweating, and shaking—are visible, and people will catch them if they're looking at you. Others don't care whether you're red or sweaty, which isn't real. It is untrue that they would hate, reject, or mock you.

The majority of people have been in situations where they have seen others seem humiliated and just ignored it. They will almost certainly sympathize with you, particularly if you seem distressed. Adolescents, who are sometimes cruel to one another and can make a big deal out of flushing or sweating, are the only exception to this rule. Other women in my practice have used a technique that one of my clients, Ingrid, used. "You will note that my neck gets all red when I talk about stuff that I have feelings about but don't worry about it," Ingrid said during our first session, avoiding any conversation about her splotchy, flushed neck. It is of no consequence. That was something that both my mother and grandmother had." By asking me not to think about the splotchiness, she catastrophizes it, and in doing so, she also stopped thinking about it. Her neck flushed, but I knew she was aware of it and had acknowledged it without hesitation, so I was able to ignore it. Her strategy was to declare it and move on.

Then again, men will, in general, experience more difficulty revealing that these side effects may happen before they do. Since women often bond with one another over trouble or embarrassing circumstances, it is easier for them to announce a flaw in advance. Men prefer to know where they stand in the hierarchy because they don't want to admit any flaws that could make them appear vulnerable in another guy's eyes. If this is the case, they may reduce their anxiety by attempting to ignore any symptoms that arise. They should remind themselves that flushing, sweating, and trembling aren't the end of the world and that staying steady with their breathing can significantly assist them. Blushers in middle or high school may need to think about more than just what to do if they show these signs of shame in front of others. They must become desensitized to the sensation of embarrassment. Meanwhile, repeat after me: "A feeling is just a feeling." It doesn't mean there's a problem" would downplay the signs and symptoms.

To recap, remember that:

- ✓ Panic is just a sensation. It's annoying, but it's not fatal. It is something to remember if you begin to feel anxious. Then try diaphragmatic breathing for a while.
- ✓ Dread is an emotion that can arise even though there is nothing wrong. The mental assertion should be reinforced; then do something to divert your focus away from the dread.
- ✓ Embarrassment is nothing more than an emotion. Make a strategy for what you'll do if you start to feel embarrassed. Remind yourself that just because you've been heard doesn't mean you'll be turned down.

"I'm going to die!" "I'm losing my mind!" "I'm losing my grip!" Even after all these years of working as a therapist for anxiety patients, it never fails to amaze me that these feelings plague virtually every panic sufferer. It would be fantastic to remind people that they are not going crazy, dying, or losing their control. The issue is that they are already aware of it. Their left prefrontal cortex knows they've been through this before and haven't died, gone insane, or lost power. Their right brain, on the other hand, is already anticipating the disaster. When fear strikes, the left brain is unable to communicate with the right brain's emotionality. The feeling is far too powerful and persuading.

I was recently reminded of this when a competent, knowledgeable man treated for panic had a panic attack relapse and ended up in the hospital. "I know it's probably just panic," he told himself, but he believed the catastrophic fear that this time it was a heart attack. Through thousands of dollars and several diagnostic examinations, his right-brain limbic structures eventually believed his left prefrontal cortex, and the fear subsided.

❖ Step 1: Find the exact image or thought you're looking for

So, what works to prevent a panic attack from being catastrophizing? Since panicking people are ordinarily unable to identify their thoughts during the panic, psychotherapy would almost certainly be needed. It's critical to be clear about what people mean when they say, "I'm dying!" "I'm going insane!" or "I'm losing control!" The first step in putting these panicky thoughts to rest is to look for this exact picture.

Let's start with "I'm dying!" Begin by recognizing the specific physical sensations that are bothering you, such as shortness of breath, chest pain, arm pain, tingling, or nausea. Then, find an exact picture of what you fear, such as falling in the street or being in a hospital's I.C.U., and play it in your mind like a movie. The majority of people have no clear vision of death. And if you imagine crashing, this isn't the end of the story, so keep going. "What happens next?" you may wonder. It is a critical topic that might be difficult to address at first. However, it's important to keep pressing to envision how the whole scenario will turn out. Keep saying, "Then what happens?" before you get to "Then I die." Then inquire, "What happens next?" once more. Most people laugh at this point, realizing that the panic is over. However, the answer to this question will reveal more about your relationships, hopes, dreams, and even what panic means to you.

Having the picture is a vital part of avoiding catastrophizing the panic symptoms for the individual who fears losing control. "What would you look like if anyone was watching you?" What will you think or do?" Take a step-by-step look at how it will seem to an outsider.

Observant. It should be done thoroughly. If you're talking about what would happen if you lost control in a public place like a bus or restaurant, you could say, "Well, I'd look scared." That, however, is insufficient. You must think about what you would look like and what you would do to the end, and then ask

yourself, "Then what?" The majority of people must learn this by meeting with a therapist who can explain their losing control images.

When I asked one of my clients, Shirley, how she would react if she lost control of the bus, she replied, "I would look terrified!" "Then what?" I wondered. Shirley looked perplexed, as though she didn't understand what I was saying, but then added, "I don't think I'd yell at the driver to let me out in the middle of the block." He'd have to pull over anyway, so I'd get off the bus as soon as possible." So I followed up with, "And what?" "People could look at me just standing on the street," Shirley thought seriously. "Then what?" I asked, and she went on to say that those people would be out of sight as the bus pulled away. "Then what?" I wondered. "I'd be stuck paying for a taxi if I tried to get to work on time!" Shirley exclaimed.

When she followed the vision of panic to the end of the scenario, she realized her fear of losing control had vanished.

The fear of "going insane" is the least likely to have a vivid, realistic picture. It's usually an expression of the fear that getting a panic attack means you're already insane. However, this isn't always the case, and it's best to stick with it until the end of the film: However, this isn't always the case, and it's best to stick with it until the end of the film: "What's going crazy?" It can be achieved in the same way as the videos of the other two fears. I did this with a client named Norman, who characterized his fear of going insane as pacing around, saying meaningless things, and waving his arms. He imagined that other people would be afraid of him and be taken to a mental institution. It seemed like a pretty good description of being "mad," It fits a lot of how he felt he looked when he was worried. Then we went on to phase 2 to thoroughly debunk his doom-and-gloom outlook.

- ❖ **Step 2: Consider whether this is similar to any other experience you've had.**

You will objectively equate the panic to the feared disaster if you remember a real experience. For example, you might be terrified of dying. It is usually brought about by physical symptoms like chest pain or shortness of breath. Finding out which symptom causes your fear of dying will help you figure out the actual cause of your fear. It often refers to someone else's disease or death. For example, a woman whose father died of a heart attack in front of her may be concerned that her chest pain is similar to her father's. When a mother

experiences shortness of breath after rushing her child to the hospital with asthma, she may feel powerless.

Understanding what you equate your panic with will assist you in desensitizing the anxiety. When I asked

Norman about his other panic attacks, he said they reminded him of his uncle, who had schizophrenia and had lived with Norman's family when Norman was a child. The uncle was always irrational and paced a lot, and he had been expelled from the house on many occasions when he "went nuts." Norman, who was just a child at the time, was terrified. Norman knew he wasn't his uncle by talking through the image of going insane, and his fear of going insane vanished.

When trauma causes catastrophic fear, the tragic fears of "going insane, losing control, or dying" are often rooted in a traumatic experience from childhood. The person who has these fears may be oblivious to stimuli in the world or relationships that set them in motion. **<u>Following these measures, you'll find out what's causing your fear:</u>**

- ✓ Keep a panic journal in which you pay close attention to the events that led up to the panic attacks.
- ✓ Look for a trend in your emotional state or the events leading up to your panic attack.

✓ Next, look for your first memory of a similar emotion or occurrence.

Identifying the source of your panic attacks will help you stop them entirely. However, identifying the cause may not be sufficient, and an individual with a history of trauma should likely seek psychotherapy to address the effects of the initial trauma. Their education and experience will determine the therapist's approach to dealing with the underlying trauma. If the source of fear cannot be identified, a psychotherapist may advise addressing the issue in counseling.

<u>To summarize, following these steps will help you debunk your panic thoughts about dying, going insane, or losing control:</u>

1. Visualize how you want this fear to play out in your head.
2. Determine whether your anxiety is justified—is it similar to some other experience you've had? Comparing your panic to the feared disaster

might be enough to break your catastrophizing habit.

3. If steps 2 and 3 don't work, look for the first time you had this anxiety or idea and see if it stemmed from a traumatic event.

4. Identifying and resolving the panic cause can require psychotherapy.

Plan to Panic

This strategy is straightforward and will help you resume the tasks you were doing before the panic attacks. It entails meticulously planning to return to circumstances where you previously panicked. It is important because, even though the circumstances themselves did not trigger the fear, it is easy to become afraid of the things you were doing when you feel panicked. When you panic when driving on a highway in the rain, your mind is so quick to make associations and so profound in its symbol construction that you are likely to be afraid of panicking the next time you drive in the rain.

As a result, you can experience panic when driving on the highway in the rain and whenever it rains or whenever you drive, regardless of how dry the road is. It's only regular for people to avoid any behavior that could cause a panic attack. Avoiding driving is popular, but people often avoid being in crowds, at large gatherings, and grocery stores during high-traffic periods of the day. They aren't social anxiety symptoms but rather a fear of panicking if you can't get away.

Preparing to panic and deal with it, rather than preparing not to panic, becomes a safety net for these conditions. In a situation where she or he has already panicked, it's difficult to avoid every potential cause of panic. So brace yourself for a panic attack.

Preparation involves simple steps

- ✓ Acquire the ability to exhale fear (technique #2).

- ✓ Go over every detail of the situation or scenario you've been avoiding.

- ✓ Desensitize yourself to every part of the situation that you are afraid of could set you off. When imagining the operation, note any aspects that made you anxious and use a technique to calm down. Systematic desensitization, **E.M.D.R.**, energy therapy, and other techniques can help you visualize and calm down before entering a situation that makes you feel anxious. (For more detail on these therapy approaches, see the Recommended Reading & Resources section.)

- ✓ Exercising. Consider staging a smaller version of the event or operation. Plan to get on a short stretch of highway at a time when it is not too busy so that you can exit and return home or go on to your destination.

- ✓ Without taking the highway, you can get to your destination. Even if the practice session is going well, finish it at the scheduled end time.

- ✓ Make a list of what you'll do if or when you start to panic. Carry your strategy on an index card or in a folder with you at all times.
- ✓ Review the strategy before entering the situation and have it on hand if you become panicked.
- ✓ Then do it for real, knowing that you have a backup plan if you panic.
- ✓ Take a look back to see how things went.
- ✓ Praise yourself for your ability to persevere in the face of adversity.
- ✓ Congratulate yourself for approaching a situation calmly.
- ✓ If you run into a crisis, figure out how you'll fix it.
- ✓ Recognize that you made it through it, no matter what happened.

Learn to Know (And Choose to Show) Anger

This technique aims to avoid catastrophizing frustration. When people think of anger as an issue, they usually think of the need to calm down and practice anger management techniques. However, rage can be so anxiety-inducing that people don't even realize they're angry—they only feel arousal and anxiety. They get rid of their fear because they don't know what they're concerned about, and in their best guesses as to why they're worried, nothing seems to work. It is because the frustration that is triggering the anxiety perception is unrecognized.

If people display their rage, they can face real dangers. They may have been hurt, abused, or emotionally rejected in the past, and the recollection of rage triggers fear. They may face similar dangers in the present: if they express their rage, they risk getting hurt or losing a friendship or work. In these cases, not being aware that you are upset becomes a useful safety valve. Unfortunately, the rage expresses itself in other forms, adding to the anxiety. As a result, it's essential to recognize it.

And if you know you're angry, you may not know how to express it. If you've never been angry before, you may not know how to express yourself adequately. You may be too quiet or blow up, which are both counterproductive. If you're aware that you're prone to outbursts of rage (anxiety can trigger some surprising outbursts of rage), you can use anger management books to help you learn to control your outbursts. There are also excellent books on assertiveness that are beneficial to people prone to extreme anger and hesitant to show anger.

6 Steps for Decatastrophizing Anger

It's not about expressing anger; it's about understanding it. And it's here where the method begins, with the promise that thinking you're upset isn't the same as showing it. It's a symptom-management technique that aims to reduce stress while increasing anger awareness. It is an easy form. Look for unrecognized rage beneath the fear when you're experiencing intense feelings of stress, concern, or stomach-squeezing doom.

1. The next time you experience intense anxiety, sit down and write as long a list as you can in single words or short phrases in response to the following question;

2. "If I were angry, what would I be angry about?" A primary aspect of the query is that it is hypothetical. You are just speculating about being upset about something on the list, so don't feel obligated to do so.

3. Consider how it felt to jot down your to-do list. What does it feel like to look at your possessions? What's the matter with your anxiety?

4. Go through the checklist one more time. Is there anything to complete on your to-do list? What are you willing to relinquish control over?

5. If you need to take action because you've been injured, taken advantage of, ignored, or worse, talk it through with others, so you don't end up in a dangerous situation. After all, you were

experiencing your frustration as fear, so you're still not used to dealing with it.

6. Developing anger-management skills could be beneficial. For people who are either hesitant or extreme in their anger speech, learning to be assertive rather than hostile is a good start.

7. After that, you can either destroy or discuss the list with your therapist. I ask my clients to talk to me about their feelings about making this list, and if they're happy, I'll listen to the whole thing. They gain insight into the relationship between anger and anxiety as they study the list and their reactions to making it. It opens the way for more in-depth psychotherapy to address clinical issues related to anger.

8. Stopping all forms of catastrophizing will help you manage your restless mind. In any case, thoughts of "No, no!" "Uh oh," or "I'm going insane!" can cause anxiety ranging from nervous tension to panic. When you practice decatastrophizing techniques, you will be able to avoid anxiety attacks before they occur.

Technique 6: Stop Anxious Thoughts

"What happens if I get too worked up?" "How am I going to get rid of these worries?" "How am I going to stand in front of other people without looking like a fool?" The anxious mind forces the sufferer to deal with the same things they fear repeatedly, and the circular nature of anxious thought affects people of all ages. Every anxious mind must master the techniques in this chapter for stopping anxious thoughts and interfering with their return if they are to learn to cope with anxiety and reduce it.

Why Do I Have So Much Trouble Stopping My Anxious Mind?

Recalling some of the brain and neurotransmitter knowledge from earlier in this chapter can help you understand what's going on with hard-to-control thoughts and why this chapter's thought-stopping techniques would function.

- ✓ Overactivity of the anterior cingulate gyrus (A.C.G.) causes worry and emotional "stuckness." It becomes essential to exercise the prefrontal cortex's (P.F.C.) decision-making power and say, "Stop!"

- ✓ The limbic system's amygdala has been conditioned to pay attention to any stimulus that may be a danger or a risk. Early in life, the amygdala can start causing worriers' problems by forming its tendency to screen for the worst.

- ✓ Increased norepinephrine (N.E.) or overactivity in the basal ganglia causes hypervigilance to errors, fear, or possible rejection or embarrassment (Pliszka, 2003). The brain is in a radar-like scanning mode, looking for signs of an issue in all incoming stimuli. To stop the "scan mode," the executive brain (P.F.C.) must prepare ahead to redirect it, which is what this technique is all about.

- ✓ When the limbic system lacks serotonin (S.E.), it leads to anxiety in the anxious brain by concentrating on what is wrong, complicated, or low.

- ✓ Serotonin (S.E.) deficiency contributes to ruminating, hopelessness, and foreseeing trouble.

Thought-Stopping and Thought Replacement

The strategy for stopping anxious thoughts consists of two parts: thought stopping and thought replacement. Thought-stopping is essential, but it's not enough. You must also focus your attention on a thinking substitute that has been prepared ahead of time. <u>Your brain decides the thoughts aren't essential and takes charge of them. Several things happen over time when the executive brain (P.F.C.) repeatedly intervenes and diverts fearful thoughts:</u>

- ✓ The ruminating and worrying anterior cingulate gyrus (A.C.G.) relaxes.
- ✓ The limbic system becomes less involved, resulting in a reduction in negative feelings.

✓ Concern has a reduced impact on the stress response.

"Self!" is the most straightforward method in the book. "Enough!"

Why is it necessary to pause our thoughts? Any repetitive thinking creates a neurobiological rut in our heads. Since it takes time to alter a neuron pathway

after it has been formed, stopping and then interrupting thoughts must be done regularly to overcome the worrying tendency. "Stop stressing! Relax!" we've all been told. He would be happy if he could stop worrying! But, to replace negative thoughts, this assertion is a crucial first step.

You tell yourself, "Self! Stop it!" while you are having out-of-control fearful thoughts. That's it. It's simply not easy. The next step—thought replacement—comes into play at this stage.

Replace Negative Thoughts

Thought replacement is the secret to effectively interrupting the concerned person's nervous cognitions. The substitute thinking must be as healthy as the negative thought, and it must be prepared ahead of time. A worrier can't wait until he or she is caught in the middle of a rumination to come up with something else to worry about. <u>What you use as a thinking replacement would simply be based on what fits your personality and style the best. There are a few different types of necessary replacements:</u>

- ✓ Switch negative, obsessed thinking for a positive one. If your anxious feelings are very obsessive, this is an excellent technique to use. In this case, the substitution should be straightforward and easily repeatable. If you're going to build a mental rut, make it a constructive one. Try reciting a scripture verse, an affirmation, a poem, or song lyrics over and over, preferably aloud. Saying the substitute aloud will add the dimension of speech and listening, occupying more of your time. While it is best to avoid encouraging rumination, there are occasions when extreme, negative rumination must be countered. An alternate, optimistic rumination may be required to defeat the negative one.

✓ Go head-to-head with your nervous feelings. Sing, talk, or recite a poem.

Making the substitute thought take up more room in your mind will increase its chances of capturing your attention. Singing activates more parts of the brain, and singing aloud activates, even more, adding the dimension of listening to optimistic thinking. Speaking or reciting the substitution aloud often gives it more control. Prepare your songs or recitation in advance.

✓ Take a break from worrying feelings. After yelling "No!"

Distract your mind away from the fear as soon as possible. Watch T.V., play video games, read, work on a hobby, call a friend (and talk about his or her life, not yours), or do something else that will take your attention away from the task at hand. Many people use their computers to entertain themselves—games, email, instant messaging, chat rooms, blogging, etc. Keep an eye on it and make sure it doesn't become obsessive, take up too much of your time, or trigger anxiety (such as if you are using it to search for information as a way to reassure yourself).

✓ Return your attention to the job or mission you were doing when the fearful thoughts first surfaced. Pay close attention to what you're doing. This thought replacement approach may be most useful at work, where singing or going for a walk may be out of the question, and staying focused on the task at hand is preferable. If the work-related activities aren't engaging enough, you may need to refocus regularly.

<u>**The easiest way to suppress worrying thoughts is to:**</u>

    i.   Remind yourself, "Self!" "Stop!" says the speaker.

    ii.   Substitute a positive thought for the negative one.

    iii.   Replacing a negative repetitive thought with a positive repetitive thought, such as an affirmation, poem, or prayer

    iv.   Is singing or reciting allowed to compete.

    v.   Is to watching television, playing video games, reading, or changing places to distract yourself.

    vi.   Refocusing on the job or task, you were doing before you became anxious.

Use the Body to Change the Mind

It can help move the body when the anterior cingulate gyrus (A.C.G.) is trapped (one source of repeated worrying thoughts). Moving and paying attention to the task will help to relieve anxiety and allow the mind to wander. There are several ways to move the body. Get up and do your job if it requires you to walk about. You may also engage in physical activity, such as walking or running while listening to music or podcasts, for added distraction. Music occupies the right side of the brain with its harmony and rhythm, pulling you farther away from fearful thoughts. When sweeping, vacuuming, or cleaning the garage, switch on some music and dance. Alternatively, you should simply dance to songs. Or, for a few minutes of constructive diversion, play some current popular video game that gets you going.

Changing places is another method for moving the brain around. Pay attention to where you're headed and what you'll be doing there as you change places. Paying conscious and deliberate attention to what you're doing now, remembering every detail, will help you make something more convincing. You're using mindfulness as a thinking substitute in this way.

Acting as an "eye witness" to notice everything around you as if something beautiful and meaningful were about to happen, and you'll be asked to explain what it looked like the moment before will help you concentrate. This degree of concentration is needed to generate enough pull to counteract the restless mind.

Although playing musical instruments necessitates movement, it is not a physically demanding activity. Other common names for kids and teens include Guitar Heroes, which is visually subtle yet emotionally compelling. Even making a **CD** mix of music to exercise or dance requires some physical activity; additionally, considering whether the music makes you want to move causes the same mental shift as the movement itself does, so it can help you relax. Making a **CD** of your favorite songs or working on a compilation of songs you'd like to share has the bonus of both cheering you up and distracting you with the activity.

When it comes to kids, moving their bodies can be very beneficial, mainly when they are nervous and display many oppositions. Before confronting them about it, suggest it. Since teenagers don't always have the self-awareness to engage in other approaches, movement is a good alternative. Determine their preferred method of movement. Music and video games that get them moving maybe their favorites. But, apart from that, what do they enjoy? In the road, shooting hoops? Are they on their bicycles? Create a list of ways you can travel while your mind is nervous, or help your anxious child or teen make one. Since

children and adolescents have more energy and need ways to release it when they are nervous, and this approach is much more necessary for adults.

The "T.W.O. P" Thought Replacement List for The Day

As the ability to substitute thoughts improves, it can become ingrained in your daily routine. Having a backup plan in place helps with both daytime and nighttime concerns. Having a regular thought replacement list based on the "Two Ps": fun and constructive is the best practice to get into for consistently battling ruminating concern. Anxiety is generally painful and ineffective, preventing you from completing any action or thought process successfully.

However, you can use your prefrontal cortex (P.F.C.) to plan specific thoughts to replace negativity and shift your restless mind to a positive state.

It functions like this:

1. Every day, spend 60 seconds identifying items you might think about during the day, such as which books to borrow from the library, which homework to complete first, which errands to run after work, which phone calls to return first, which Hawaiian Island to visit first on vacation, and so on. Any thoughts that aren't fun or constructive should be excluded from the list. Use a single reminder word for each thought to write down these fun or productive thoughts on a post-it note or index card. Since these ideas are likely to change regularly, make a list every morning for one minute.

2. Post the list on a workplace bulletin board, clipboard, phone, car dashboard, computer monitor, wallet, or pocket—anywhere it would be readily accessible.

3. Check the "Two P" list for a substitution to distract your mind as soon as you've stopped rumination with thought stopping.

4. Continue this process regularly until rumination is no longer an issue.

It takes time to calm rumination, and this simple method will help you remain productive without creating new ruminative thoughts.

By interrupting fearful thoughts, this crucial yet fundamental approach has a positive impact on the entire brain.

<u>Still, keep in mind that</u>

- A hyperactive limbic system causes negativity.
- Rumination is caused by the anterior cingulate gyrus (A.C.G.) inability to transmit information to the prefrontal cortex (P.F.C.) for resolution.
- The P.F.C.'s preparation and conscious focus practices are responsible for suppressing negative, obsessive thinking. You may help the P.F.C. actively move the A.C.G. away from the

nervous thinking by creating and using a list of replacement thoughts. It will help suppress the limbic system's overactivity by allowing it to calm down (Schwartz, 1996).

Non-verbal Reminders of Thought Replacement for Kids and Others

When anxiety strikes, not everyone remembers what they were going to think as a substitute thought, and not everyone works well with a list. Nonverbal reminders come in handy in these situations. Here are some ideas about making reminders for how you want to replace worry until you say, "Self! Stop It!":

- ✓ An interactive flip map. Create a thinking substitute reminder book with a three-ring binder or a spiral notebook. Draw an image, write a sign, stick a sticker, or paste or tape a magazine or newspaper cutout onto a notebook page if you have a good idea. When you're looking for mental or physical activity to replace your thoughts, look through your notebook before you find one that suits the bill. It is beneficial for both children and individuals who are more visual in their responses.

✓ A symbol card for the classroom or the office, a necessary card that can be kept on or in your desk at school or work, can be used to incorporate the idea of a reminder notebook with icons or visual clues. For small children, stickers or markers can be used—for example, a small picture of the family dog can be a reminder of something fun to think about, or a book sticker can be a reminder that the child can read a book for diversion. Workplace stations can use an adult version of the same types of reminders about friends, family, pets, and activities.

✓ Pictures of happy places (vacation destinations, beloved people, or pets) can be shown on a bulletin board or desk, or a magnet can be used to tape them to the refrigerator.

✓ These symbols and nonverbal reminder ideas can be prepared in therapy, using teachers or parents, and so on.

The Second-Easiest Method in The Book: Do the Worst First

This simple technique will go a long way toward calming the restless mind. Do the worst first is a clear reminder to do what you don't want to do, but need to do as soon as possible. If you're going to be worried all day about something you have to do (like make a phone call you don't want to make or pay your bills), do it first and spare yourself the stress. What a relief it is! It is remarkably effective at permanently relaxing the restless mind. When you have a negative thought on your mind, it agitates you. Anxiety causes the brain to fear more and more. However, once you complete this mission, your brain will be able to relax. The longer you can keep your brain calm, the easier it will be to keep your brain calm. This approach works well in everyday scenarios, including calling a disgruntled customer or returning a faulty item to the store when you don't want to deal with the operation. It can also be used for laundry, homework, or writing a working paper.

While this approach is useful for the minor issues that arise at work and home regularly, it is also useful for severe, significant issues. Throughout their lives, most people will be confronted with significant problems. Real issues would undoubtedly necessitate a commitment to suitable solutions, but worriers are also very adept at dealing with them. Indecision and uncertainty irritate the brain, exacerbating anxiety.

Stuff like telling someone you've seen for a long time that you're ending your relationship, telling a buddy you think he's drinking too much. Confronting a partner about lying to you, talking to your child about having drugs in her home, and other similar issues drag us down. They occupy our anxious minds and divert our attention away from other things. You were correcting your beliefs about doing the worst first aids in your motivation to do so.

<u>**Try the following procedure:**</u>

1. Can you recall when you were faced with a similar challenge and how relieved you felt when you completed it? Bring that relaxation to your mind. If you're putting off a chore, think about how much you enjoy it when the bathroom is clean, how you felt lighter after telling your buddy you weren't going to the concert you didn't want to pay for. Or how relaxing it felt doing something you wanted to do took your mind off the job or the problem.

2. Calculate how much time you've got until you have to do something you don't want to do. Consider how much the job will weigh on your mind for all those hours.

3. Think to yourself, "Do I want to be worried about it for all those hours, or do I want those hours to be hours of relief?"

4. If you immediately do the dreaded thing, pay close attention to the advantages so you can recall them the next time you need to

remember why doing the worst first is a good idea. Pay attention to how many hours you feel bad, nervous, or anxious if you do not do what you fear or put it off until the last minute. Consider if the doing was as painful as you expected and whether the relief of having it done was worth the hours of waiting.

While you will need some time to consider it, getting the worst of it out of the way as soon as possible allows you to step forward rather than sitting on the razor's edge of fear, attempting to be relaxed but suffering no matter how you place yourself. The sooner you get off the brink and do what you've been putting off, the sooner you'll feel better, and your restless mind will be free.

Make A List with Time Frames

Holly was convinced she was suffering from a panic attack. "I'm not sure how I'm going to finish it all!" I'm having trouble breathing, and it's making me so anxious." Holly was nearing the end of her master's worry to see if it requires more attention is beneficial when dealing with these concerns. Continue asking yourself, "Is there anything else I should be concerned about?" until you get a negative response. The only way for the worried mind to move on is to do so. By ensuring that all possibilities are protected, this move avoids worrying later on. When you say you're already worried, your brain has to believe you, and it'll believe you more readily if you ask this question purposefully while you're already worried.

5. Schedule a time when you'll need to revisit the worry, and write it down somewhere: "If x happens, I'll do y." If x does not occur, I will revisit this concern on March 15th." (Write "Worry about X" in your calendar.) It will free the

2. nervous mind from remembering when to be concerned, as it would otherwise do. You can say, "I know when to worry again, and I don't

have to worry now," after writing a "worry date" into the calendar.

6. Declare, "Stop! I'm already worried!" if the concern arises again, and use thought substitution strategies to redirect your thoughts as quickly as possible.

The challenge for Noelle was to focus on changing her manager rather than worrying about how to do so. It was a way of saying, "Well, let's think about what would happen if you lose your job," as if it had already happened. We started by laying out all of the potential sources of her concern. <u>Her only concern seemed to be "What if I lose my job?" at first, but she was gradually able to split that concern down into several components:</u>

- ✓ If I lose my career, how can I make ends meet?
- ✓ Where'd I find another job?
- ✓ What if I'm out of work for the rest of my life?

Then we went on to phase 2, which was to complete any tasks that needed to be completed as quickly as possible. Noelle dialed her boss's number and told him that she would be available on Wednesday evening. She also wanted to establish a tight work schedule for the future, which she addressed with her boss. It only partially alleviated her worries of being shot. The third phase, creating a plan, was then required.

Noelle came up with two solutions to her concern about paying her rent if she lost her job. She'd first approach her mother and request a loan. Second, as she searched for another career, she would apply for a nearby grocery store job. We spoke about her concerns before she came up with a strategy for dealing with them. "Do you have something else to be concerned about?" I asked Noelle. For a few minutes, she pondered. "What would I do if I am shot and lose my health insurance? Without health insurance, I can't function!" We talked about a solution once more. Noelle learned about COBRA's continuity health plan and how to qualify for it.

Following that, Noelle set a date on her calendar to deal with this issue in the future. She agreed it was fair to revisit her concern about holding her job once a month if her boss's attitude changed noticeably, and she scheduled a worry session for the 15th of the month.

Finally, Noelle thought like she had worried enough about the issue, at least for the time being, after all of this preparation. "Stop!" she told herself as her anxiety flared up again. I'm still worried!" she exclaimed, recalling that she'd scheduled a reassessment for the 15th. Then she used thought substitution methods to divert her attention away from the issue.

The "worry well and only once" approach aims to combat the temptation to develop new worries. Using the PFC roles of research and decision-making to their full potential means taking the time to discover all facets of a problem. So, they can be analyzed ("Do I need a strategy or not?") and addressed ("When or under what conditions should I revisit my worry?"). Since the cortex has purposefully modulated the program and preparing to begin her first full-time job. She also needed to complete some coursework and pack her apartment. There were also several minor tasks to complete before the ceremony, such as submitting her degree paperwork and receiving her robe. She admitted to being a shamble. "A week!" she exclaimed when I asked how much time she had to do this stuff. I realized that a list was necessary.

Making a list to relieve anxiety entails more than just writing down what needs to be done, but it is an excellent place to start. Making a list entails calculating how long each task will take and determining what is most important. When you know exactly how much you can accomplish in a day, you can set realistic goals for yourself. The decision about what to do when eliminates the uncertainty of what

will be accomplished, and the nervous self-talk about not doing enough or doing it correctly.

I asked Holly to take a deep breath before handing her a pad of paper and instructing her to jot down anything she wanted to do. We worked on this list together out loud because I wanted to make sure she was thorough. It proved to be a wise decision. <u>The phrase "pack the apartment" morphed into a longer list:</u>

- ✓ Layout all of the clothes I'll need for the week
- ✓ Pack up the rest of my belongings.
- ✓ Make sure I have all of my plates, pots, and pans with me.
- ✓ Pack the toiletries in a packet.
- ✓ Pack all of my linens and bedding in a crate.

We determined that some of her tasks would be errands, and others would be items she wanted to do at home, so she divided her list into errands and home tasks, which I'd be handy later when she was deciding when and how to complete the job. She then added the small and large tasks of wrapping up the school-related specifics of graduation to the list. She also recalled a few more minor tasks, such as returning keys, that she would have remembered later—probably just as she was beginning to relax from her panic.

The next move was to go through each item on the list and determine how long each would take her in minutes. Turn in the keys seemed to be a minor task, but driving to her landlord and returning home would take 45 minutes unless she could combine it with another errand (which she subsequently did). She then proceeded to provide a time estimate for each item on the list. She then organized all of the tasks into a hierarchy, starting with the most important and working her way down. It is the phase in which you will be able to relax and feel less anxious. Knowing how realistically you can do a short period relieves the burden of the stuff that won't get done if you only have a limited amount of time. You can relax about anything else if your primary and most important activity of the day is to finish your homework (or the job you took home), and you know it will take about 90 minutes. You can do something else without thinking about finishing your homework because you know you'll have 90 minutes after dinner to finish it. You may also divert your attention to something else because you know you only have 90 minutes, which is insufficient time to complete another task. Holly had more than one day, so after making her list, she calculated how much time she had left on each day and started plugging in the tasks, starting with the most important and working her way down to the least important. She had to work with some fixed appointments and schedule time for lunch and other breaks.

Her anxiety dissipated when she learned she had about two days' worth of work and seven days to complete it. She couldn't get through that because she was so frustrated by the number of activities. In that state of agitation, she would have been less efficient. She was now considering how she would spend her final week before starting her new job.

When people do this for a day's worth of work, they usually get a completely different result than Holly. It was the case for John, who made a to-do list before going on holiday with his dad. He found he had 1012 hours of work to do and just 8 hours to complete it, so he had to reduce his aspirations by 212 hours. He then determined which tasks on his to-do list were essential and which tasks could be skipped. So, rather than expecting a stressful day, he felt relaxed, knowing he had time to prepare for his departure. He could make a new list if everything didn't go as expected, so unless that happened, he'd be able to complete his tasks without feeling rushed, which is what makes days like today so stressful.

Making lists will also help you avoid the frustration that comes with being late for an appointment, meeting, or social event. The list can be mentally completed in under a minute to see if you can, for example, stop at the store, the dry cleaner, and the pharmacy on the way to pick up the kids after baseball practice. Even if you know you'll have to miss one of the activities, you'll feel less agitated, which is good for relaxing the restless mind.

<u>To summarize how making a list will help you avoid anxious thoughts:</u>

1. 1. Create a list of activities that must be completed.

2. Calculate how long each job will take (including time spent driving, walking, or taking the bus).

3. Sort things in your list priority order.

4. Remove tasks that you won't be able to complete with the time you have available.

The Technique for Stopping Thoughts in Its Tracks

Persistence is key when it comes to avoiding thoughts. Symptoms are normally permanent, and the technique only works if it is used regularly.

Therapists working with generalized anxiety people will go through this material, again and again, to pick up on all the subtleties of their thought process and strengthen thought replacement techniques. This procedure takes a long time to complete. Improvement can be seen almost immediately, but it can take weeks, if not months, for the restless mind to become consistently calm.

The trick to getting thought-stopping to work as quickly as possible is to try to distract thoughts regularly. If the thought-blocking techniques are only used on occasion, progress would be slow. When you first start practicing thought-stopping, you may notice a brief rise in fearful thoughts (this is more likely when the thoughts are both recurrent and consistent), but a rapid reduction in worrying will accompany this.

There is a clear connection between using this approach regularly and reducing brain overactivity. Janis, one of the most dedicated therapists I've ever seen, exemplifies the importance of perseverance. Janis, who was plagued by anxious thoughts during counseling, used every technique I recommended—a very rare client! Her ruminations about whether her cancer would recur were constant and highly distressing. She could use thought-stopping to disrupt these thoughts now that she had learned to relax her body. She announced progress after just a week, and she said the secret to making it work was my warnings about how difficult it would be to remain persistent. "I thought you were joking when you said I'd have to think-stop every time the cancer thought came up, even though it happened a thousand times a day," she explained. If you hadn't warned me, I would have given up after around 100 attempts on the first day, convinced that this approach would never work for me. But because you said 1,000 times a day, I thought I should keep going." What a great example of persevering in the face of adversity!

Thought-stopping comes first in the process of calming mental fear. Learning to relax the nervous system is the first step. The bad news is that unlike physical relaxation, which can be achieved quickly, relaxing the restless mind and avoiding anxious thoughts requires time and practice. The good news is that the anxious brain's high energy can be harnessed to redirect successfully. Make a conscious effort to replace your anxious emotions with more optimistic ones. Make a conscious effort to replace your anxious emotions with more optimistic ones.

Technique 7: Contain Your Worry

Everyone worries, but people who suffer from generalized anxiety make it an art form. They transform ordinary concerns into monstrous impediments to critical thought, exaggerating them out of proportion to reality by unnecessary rumination. The restless mind can even get stuck on strange things like violating rules, germs and contagion, poisoning, and inadvertently harming others. This exaggeration of normal concern could lead to hysteria or delusion, leading people to believe they're going insane.

This type of concern is difficult to manage; it becomes an anxiety disorder as it consumes a person's life and prevents them from paying attention to the details that enrich or inform their lives. When a person can no longer ignore worry, it's time to take control and learn how to deal with it. No one can completely escape anxiety; however, everyone can manage it. This approach recognizes that people can't always "stop thinking about it," as their family and friends advise. Instead, they must learn how to manage their anxieties.

The techniques in this technique will not only offer immediate relief from worry. They will also change the probability of future concern by calming down the overactive limbic system, which overreacts to signs of trouble with excessive worry. Like the others, this approach aims to reduce the frequency, severity, and length of anxiety symptoms to give the anxious brain a break. The anxious mind will recover from its agitation and produce less anxiety until it is free of anxiety symptoms.

What's Making You So Worried?

The anterior cingulate gyrus (ACG) is being clogged by that pesky negative, limbic-generated concern! Low serotonin levels increase negativity, frustration, and the energy needed to control worry, making the prefrontal cortex (PFC) too exhausted to take command. Worry comes back to bother you even though your mind is momentarily distracted, like a raspberry seed stuck in your molar that your tongue is desperately trying to get rid of. This technique requires the PFC to perform a manual override on the automated mechanism.

When people are worried like this, psychotherapy can be very helpful because the anxiety appears very real to those who are trapped. They lose sight of all the reasons why it is not necessary to be concerned. It's similar to using a tow truck to get a perfectly working vehicle out of a ditch if they need assistance getting out of their rut. The car is in perfect working order, except that it cannot steer or drive forward while its wheels are spinning. If the car is out of the rut, it will return to its previous road-handling level. Worry management helps the brain to focus on its tasks instead of spinning its wheels. Carrie could spend an entire day worrying about the tiniest danger. Carrie, a college senior, was interviewing for positions and had to fit them in with her classes and work. She had one interview planned that was a long drive from campus, but she figured she'd be able to make it and be back in time for her senior seminar—a once-a-week class she couldn't skip without impacting her final score. "What if the ride takes you too long?" her amygdala warned after she overheard two classmates discussing construction beginning on the highway she would need to drive. Then her mind became engrossed in fear of missing the interview.

When she was able to shake that off, her thoughts would shift to being late for work. Since she thought the implications would be bad, her reasoning never entered to consider what the real consequences would be. She eventually told me she was stumped and had been worried for a week. She was very upset, and she was losing control of or correcting her anxieties.

Much of her anxiety could be alleviated by preparation, but not all of it could. Even if there was no construction, she could be late for the interview or class since highway delays caused by accidents or bad weather can happen at any time. She had to learn to keep her anxiety in check.

Get the Right Reassurance

People can attempt to conceal or eliminate ruminating anxiety rather than confronting it head-on. They also try to do this by finding proof that their fears are unfounded. They believe that if they only hear the right stuff, they will be

relieved of their anxiety. They constantly seek clarification from others that they have nothing to be concerned about. They want to be reassured once and for all, and they sometimes hear information that provides them with relief—at least temporarily.

On the other hand, the worried mind will eventually find a reassurance weakness, and there will always be something in it that makes it suspicious or ineffective. The restless mind would then embark on a new quest for solace. It is why searching the Internet has become such a time-consuming pastime for anxious people. They should look for reassurance without troubling their families and friends. Reassurance-seeking is a trap that exacerbates anxiety while failing to show you how to stop worrying in the future.

Worriers like this may even have strange thoughts that they are aware are strange but can't seem to get rid of. They can't get reassurance unless they mention these feelings, but they don't want to reveal the essence of their (irrational) concern. Let's say a worrier is concerned that she has been exposed to a particularly dangerous form of tuberculosis that was recently highlighted in the news after a man who knew he had it traveled abroad.

<u>The anxious person may seek reassurance in one of the following ways:</u>

- ✓ She might joke, "I'm going to keep my boarding pass in my safe deposit box because if it turns out I have that TB, I want to be sure I can prove I was on his plane and join the class action suit."
- ✓ She might remark, such as, "I bet I sat next to that guy—the passenger next to me coughed the

whole flight." That'll teach me never to fly without a surgical mask!"

✓ She could pose a question, such as, "Isn't there any chance the airline wouldn't call to tell me he's on my flight?" What the worrier receives in response can provide some relief or cause a new round of anxiety.

An individual searching the Internet for a potential reason for his recurring headaches, for example, could come across a slew of frightening possibilities, each of which adds to his list of concerns.

Reassurance that the worrier is capable of dealing with issues is the correct reassurance. The incorrect reassurance implies that "everything will be fine," which the restless mind will only believe for a brief moment before shifting to new concerns. Brandon is an excellent example. After a long bike ride, he developed chafing marks at the juncture of his hip and thigh, and he was concerned that he had an STD. He realized he hadn't had the marks before the trip, but his mind came up with a long list of excuses why this might be an indication of STD trouble. He reasoned that if he only dialed the STD information toll-free number, he'd get enough information to stop worrying. When he called, he was assured that the symptoms he was concerned about were unrelated to a sexually transmitted disease. "Wow!" said his PFC to his limbic system, sending a soothing massage. "Thank you so much!" However, the friendly voice on the other end of the line advised him that STD signs do not always show right away and might not be noticeable in a sexual partner, so if he had sexual intercourse with someone who may have had an STD, he should see his doctor regardless. "Red alert!" his amygdala yelled at him. I may be suffering from symptoms and be completely unaware of them!" It didn't matter what his real risk was; he was given the incorrect guarantee. He overheard something that prompted another needless concern while finding reassurance about his chafed skin. Worriers who strive to escape distress by seeking reassurance for every concern are more likely to experience this.

<u>**Brandon was in desperate need of some reassuring words. Reassurance in the right way consists of:**</u>

1. It is getting the anxiety out in the open to see if it's a real issue. The majority of good worriers are unable to distinguish between their worry and the real thing. When the real thing is put in front of them, they normally recognize it and react appropriately. On the other hand, they have no way of knowing if their fears are justified. Brandon's first impressions were positive. He called the hotline because he couldn't figure out whether he had a real problem and wanted to know if there was something he could do about it.

2. Ascertaining that a person is capable of dealing with the potential problem's consequences. Brandon's situation deteriorated at this point. Instead of being told that if he contracted an STD, he would be capable of figuring out what to do about it, he told him that he was incapable of even realizing he had a problem. He needed to hear that he could figure out

a plan that would allow him to (a) identify an STD and (b) seek treatment.

3. The most important thing is to assure that the worrier knows how to control and stop worrying. Brandon could have contained his anxiety for a day or two if he had managed his worry better, allowing the chafing to subside and not allowing his anxiety to take over.

Panic and Social Anxiety: The Correct Reassurance

In contrast to generalized anxiety, the correct reassurance for panic and social anxiety is a little different. When people are concerned about panicking or blowing it in a social situation, they should answer their concerns head-on because it's almost all about whether they'll display their symptoms and how others will respond. If they can get the anxiety out on the table, it would be beneficial to them. Hearing them admit that they are afraid of how they would appear or behave if they develop symptoms may be comforting. It is a concern that can be answered by assuring the anxiety sufferer of their ability to cope. <u>It is a concern that can be answered by assuring the anxiety sufferer of their ability to cope. When you're feeling anxious, the best thing you can do is:</u>

1. Recognize that the anxiety you're feeling is a fear of panic.
2. Remind the panicked person (or yourself) of the coping skills they already possess.

The prospect of having a panic attack can be terrifying. It's what makes us stop panic-inducing conditions. Hearing the good reassurance may also be helpful. Rather than saying, "Oh, you won't panic," say, "Even if you panic, you'll get through it." Alternatively, "Even if you panic, once it passes, you can resume your previous activities." Alternatively, "When you panic, even if it's a lot of panics, you have all the resources you need to deal with it." Of course, if you use this last example, the individual will need panic-reduction skills like diaphragmatic breathing and cued relaxation.

<u>People who suffer from social anxiety are often more likely to be afraid of their anxiety symptoms, particularly if they are noticeable to others. For social anxiety, the best reassurance is:</u>

1. Write down all your problems on paper. What are your predictions for the future?

2. Ascertain that they are capable of dealing with their fears' distress.

3. Ascertain that they are capable of dealing with the circumstances that they are afraid of. If the fear is of doing something new and looking scared when doing it, two competency levels are required: skills and anxiety management. Check to see if the individual is capable of dealing with the situation. People who suffer from social anxiety often need to re-learn social skills that they may have overlooked as children. They don't think they'll be able to deal with anxiety in a social environment beyond their ability and experience.

4. Convince them that they are capable of dealing
    with their anxiety and its consequences.

In any case, reassurance should be provided only once. It is a disguised form of worrying if an individual repeatedly expresses the same concern. For any particular concern or situation that someone brings up, the rule should be "one time through." For example, if a woman is having trouble reacting to her mother-in-criticisms law's and keeps bringing it up, she is most likely looking for reassurance. She may seek reassurance about how to deal with her Thanksgiving dinner's mother-in-criticism laws and then seek reassurance about how to deal with the mother-in-criticism laws of her birthday party hosting the following week. It is the same concern, so there is no need to go over it again.

It is not necessary to repeat a situation after it has been checked using the measures outlined above. If the concern returns, reassuring words are simple: "You know how to deal with anxiety and can handle being worried or scared."

<u>To summarize, the following is a list of appropriate reassurance for each of the three anxiety types:</u>

<u>Concerns in general:</u>

1. Get the worry out in the open and see if it's a genuine concern or just a worry.
2. If there is a genuine problem, devise a strategy that reinforces trust in your ability to solve it.
3. If it's a concern, bring it to a halt and keep it contained.
4. Assuage the anxiety-ridden person by saying, "You are capable of managing your anxiety."

<u>Anxiety:</u>

1. Recognize that the anxiety you're experiencing is a fear of panic.
2. Remind the person of their coping abilities.
3. Assuage the anxious person by saying, "You are capable of dealing with your panic and its consequences."

<u>To help with social anxiety, try these suggestions.</u>

1. Write down all of your worries on a piece of
   paper.

2. Make a strategy for dealing with any practical
   elements that might arise, such as acquiring
   new skills or practicing existing ones if
   necessary.

3. Repeat the strategies to deal with anxiety
   before and during a situation to ensure that
   you have all the requisite coping skills.

4. Inform the frightened individual that they can
   deal with their anxiety and the effects of their
   fear.

<u>Anxiety in all its forms:</u>

It is not necessary to repeat a scene after it has been
checked. If the concern returns, reassuring words are
simple: "You know how to deal with anxiety and can
handle being worried or scared."

The Antidote to Worrying Is Planning.

When people confidently take action to solve their problems, worry is defeated. I've discovered that people concerned about things going wrong are often adept at dealing with them when they do. The ambiguity of potential problems is what makes anxiety so difficult for people. Because real problems have real solutions, they don't cause anxiety about what to do about them. To an anxious mind, a clear plan of action is a godsend. Even though people with anxiety may perform better when confronted with real problems rather than worries, they may struggle with planning. They may also be unable to see how they can use the plan to alleviate anxiety. Planning is a simple but undervalued skill that can go a long way toward calming a meditative mind. You will be at a loss for how to get relief if you lack planning skills. If you're worried about an upcoming situation, see if you can devise a strategy to deal with it. A typical scenario would be a type of worry about "what if." "What if my car breaks down while I'm on vacation?"

"What if I don't pass the exam?" "What if no one invites me to the prom?" "What if I don't get the job for which I applied?"

There's one thing that all of these scenarios have in common: if they occur, a response will be necessary, and in each case, they can devise a plan. Worriers are unable to distinguish between what may require action and what is merely a cause of worry. Ensuring you know how to make a plan and then seeing if the situation is something for which a plan can be made is a great way to deal with the "what if" syndrome. Problem-solving and planning skills can be taught using a variety of resources. (A quick Internet search for books on problem-solving and planning skills yields a long list of options for various age groups and types of settings.) How to clarify the problem is always one of the first things a plan addresses. If you can't think of a specific problem that it can solve, it's probably just a worry, and stopping and replacing your thoughts will suffice. It will be a relief to the anxious mind if you can identify a problem and then make a plan. Anxiety is induced by "what if" thinking. The goal of thought-stopping is to calm the anxious mind by removing the arousal of constant anxiety. As a result, deciding what to do if a problem arises becomes part of the overall strategy of not thinking about it. The idea is to never think about the "what if" cognitions again once they've been identified and resolved into action plans, unless they happen, in which case the anxious person has a plan in place. If you find yourself worrying again, command it to stop by saying, "Stop!" I have a plan!" and then, without looking at the plan, replace the "what if" with a thought replacement that was planned ahead of time.

Making a good plan entails the following steps:

1. It clearly defines the problem, including when it will become a problem and how you will know if a solution is required.

2. Provide a list of potential solutions to the problem (brainstorming).

3. Taking into consideration all of the possibilities (you may need a pro-con list here).

4. It is deciding on a course of action.

5. Make a list of the steps you'll take to carry out your strategy.

6. When it's time to put the strategy into action, get started on it and stick to it.

7. It is assessing the effectiveness of the strategy.

It's easier to recall the strategy if you write it down. The knowledge is reintroduced to your mind by a different route when you see the list written down.

Now let's look at these steps to decide the problem at hand.

A good plan begins with a description of the issue. It may seem like a no-brainer, but it is the most crucial step. Because the problem shifts as you worry, "what ifs" can indefinitely go on in your head. For example, "What if I'm not invited to the prom?" "What if I'm asked by someone I don't like?" becomes a possibility. "What if I ask anyone who says no?" "What if I say yes to someone because I'm afraid no one else will, and then someone I like asks me?" "What if I don't have anyone to go with two weeks, a week, two days before... When am I going to take action?" It could go on indefinitely. Now's the time to call a day! Describe this problem. Even though all of the "what ifs" in this scenario seem interesting, they are only issues if you are invited to the prom. The solution is to deal with the question, "What if I'm not asked?" with a plan. "What if I am asked?" is a question you can answer by saying, "I will pause and devise a new plan."

Brainstorm Options

It's time to brainstorm after you've determined the true nature of the problem. Brainstorming entails quickly considering a variety of options in the event of a crisis. During this stage, don't censor yourself; write down everything that comes to mind, even if it seems ridiculous. Now is the time to keep your mind active and stimulate your creativity. Do you recall how the anterior cingulate gyrus (ACG) becomes stuck? Finding as many solutions as possible is an intentional (PFC) way to get unstuck in problem-solving. You might even want to enlist the help of someone else— his or her perspective will be unique, and he or she may be able to spark new ideas. After you've compiled a long list of options, you can start weighing them against each other using a pro-con list.

Option 1:

In addition to assisting the ACG in getting unstuck, listing all of the options, including the ridiculous and outrageous ones, facilitates the process of choosing the best one. Seeing the apparent mistakes makes it easier to recognize and accept the correct decision. Assume you are dissatisfied with your work and have considered your options. You've mentioned the option of "quitting today," even though you know it's ridiculous. You say, "Of course I won't leave." "The money I earn is necessary for me." However, it would help if you left, and writing it down demonstrates that you have options. Staying seems better now that you know you have a choice. It also clarifies what the rest of the choices are. Finally, listing all is essential because crazy ideas may often sow the seeds of viable solutions. Seeing a few "best" choices is generally fairly easy. Finding the best of that party, on the other hand, may necessitate a pro-con list or a cost-benefit analysis. Again, writing it down makes the decisions more obvious. Furthermore, since the anxious mind has difficulty focusing, writing things down will help concentrate attention on Without the most critical elements of the approach wandering off into the territory of more uncertainty on which option to select.

Another very popular explanation for getting stuck at this stage is that you're running out of time. The restless mind yearns for a perfect decision. You won't have to worry if you can find the perfect choice. (Recall how perfectionism is a defense mechanism against anxiety? It's also available in this form.) "There are many nice options," remind yourself. "There isn't such a thing as the ideal solution." Then choose one of the strong ones to execute.

The planning process on that issue is completed until the plan is chosen and measures for following the plan are written down. Worriers who worry about "what if" can quickly switch to "What if I didn't think of everything?" and continue to worry by replanning the plan they just made. "Stop!" you must exclaim as soon as this happens. I've got a plan!" and then, for whatever reason, divert your attention away from the plan. Even going over your strategy again to convince yourself that you have one is a type of "what if" thought that must be stopped if you want to reduce your anxiety.

Examine the Plan's Effectiveness The amygdala, the part of the brain that is constantly on the lookout for danger, requires opportunities to understand that certain things do not have to be frightening or anxiety-inducing. The amygdala gets a chance to see if a new scenario differs from an old one when you make a plan. Taking the time to assess a situation's outcome will aid the process.

A prefrontal cortex (PFC) decision to interpret all of the information coming from the senses and the body through the limbic system bring conscious attention to the result. It requires the anterior cingulate gyrus

(ACG) to process motivational information from the basal ganglia and integrate the orbit frontal cortex. The entire brain participates. If you take the time to study or not, the amygdala would have learned something, but it will learn a lot more if you do it deliberately.

It is possible to relive a situation by recalling all of its information. Reliving it helps to strengthen its memory, and concentrating on the good result helps reinforce the anxiety desensitization that happens when things go according to plan. Even if the outcome isn't perfect, note which parts of the solution worked and which didn't let you feel and analyze what worked, instead of getting lost in fear of what didn't. Many worried people ignore something that isn't flawless as useless. Evaluating results can help you escape perfectionism by allowing you to see that there can be a lot of good in a solution's few flaws.

If never implemented a problem solution and its action plan because it never arose, should note that outcome. It reaffirms the fact that the vast majority of our fears are unfounded. Those "what ifs" are just possibilities, not facts.

<u>To summarize, the following is the plan:</u>

1. Look for "what if" scenarios that can be addressed with a strategy.
2. Figure out what's wrong.
3. Make a list of possible solutions and choose one that is good—no solution is ideal.
4. If possible, write down the steps you'll take.
5. Tell yourself, "Stop!" when you start worrying about "what if." "I've devised a strategy!" exclaims the speaker.
6. Start thinking differently right now.
7. The schedule should not be re-planned.
8. When it's time to use the strategy, put it into effect.
9. Determine whether or not you followed through with the strategy.

Noelle was concerned about her job security. She was still aware of her boss's moods and commented on her job security to her sister on a near-daily basis. "Well, he looked at me funny when I told him I wanted Wednesday night off," she would say, "and I'm sure he's just waiting to see if I'll be able to work overtime to make up for it." I'm sure I'll be in huge trouble if I don't succeed." Noelle's sister suggested she see a therapist after noticing she was having anxiety problems.

I started thinking about potential reasons for Noelle's issue when she explained it to me. She might be struggling with her self-esteem or reading other people's emotions. She may be overreacting to small cues from her supervisor that her request is causing him trouble. Noelle may have been hypervigilant in the absence of a personality disorder, perceiving her job situation as "precarious" when she was the one who was unsure of her boss's attitude. In the absence of evidence, she may have been concerned. However, if a real danger exists, worrying about losing your job is fair. I couldn't be sure if her employer decided to fire her, so any effort to persuade her just to stop worrying was futile.

Furthermore, simply stopping one's thoughts would be insufficient because a new threat could emerge every day. If Noelle didn't want to take her insecurity and wear her sister out, she needed to learn how to handle her job concerns once and for all. It was the perfect opportunity to show her how to "worry well and just once." It is a tactic for dealing with worry just once. It distinguishes between legitimate concerns and irrational fears. It entails assessing what you can manage versus what you can't and what you can influence versus what you can't. It also aids you in making plans for when it is appropriate to be concerned once more.

There should be a time limit on worrying, well, just only. It usually only takes 10 to 15 minutes.

1. List the things that you want to get rid of that could make you anxious. Brainstorm to ensure that you have answered all your questions and that nothing is left behind until later. Dissect each worry in detail.

2. Complete any tasks that need to be completed right now. Make phone calls, talk to someone, write or make something, fix, clean, or do something else to improve the situation.

3. In some situations, taking action is only needed if an issue arises.

1. Making a plan is an intermediate phase where you can't put a dilemma aside, where planning skills can help. Examine the situation and devise a strategy for dealing with it if it occurs.

4. Ask yourself, "Is there anything else in this situation that I should be concerned about?" If you answered yes, proceed to the steps for determining whether or not you have a real problem that requires a solution and a deadline. If it doesn't, it's classified as worrying without a strategy. Setting a date to revisit the

concern and can remember doing so, the whole brain will respond by calming down faster while doing thought-stopping on the issue later. Over time, halting and replacing thoughts about the issue will relax the rest of the brain's operation.

<u>In summary,</u>

1. Contemplate all of the problems at hand.
2. Do whatever you need to do right now to relieve your anxiety and not put it off any longer.
3. Create a contingency plan in case some elements of the issue resurface at a later date.
4. Ask yourself, "Do I need to be concerned about anything else?"
5. Schedule another time to reflect on the anxiety.
6. Then say, "Stop!" if the idea arises. I'm concerned already!"

Technique 8: Control TMA (Too Much Activity)

Anxiety characterized by stress, worry, and high-drive behavior is exacerbated by too much activity (TMA), leading to a nonstop lifestyle that they cannot alter. Many with a sensitive disposition who are easily overstimulated are more likely to avoid this lifestyle because they know TMA's draining effects on their energy and focus. They quickly learn how much more anxious they get when they try to do too much. However, the worrier, who suffers from generalized anxiety, thrives on movement and is less likely to notice its negative consequences. While people with panic disorder may also have TMA, the person with high tension and drive is more likely to have TMA-related issues.

The Brain and TMA

If the anterior cingulate gyrus (ACG) is low on serotonin, it becomes "stuck." High-drive people don't seem to be able to determine if they should let go of something until they've started doing it. They are unable to see any viable options. It increases the chances of them increasing their workload rather than learning new skills like delegation and prioritization.

Elevated norepinephrine (NE) is related to perfectionism, linked to depression and hypervigilance in generalized anxiety. Perfectionism is linked to elevated norepinephrine (NE), which is associated with the stress and hypervigilance of generalized anxiety. TMA is exacerbated by the need to prevent errors. The braking system of the brain, GABA, may be inadequate or ineffective in some situations. It also leads to TMA by making it difficult for the person to put things away and maintain perspective mentally. It complicates the relaxation process. Worrying is challenging to avoid when GABA isn't functioning correctly, which exacerbates perfectionism is a personality trait that many people have perfectionism.

Overactivity in the basal ganglia (BG) may lead to highly driven, goal-directed actions, and people with that motivation can get a lot done in a day, no matter what they're doing—washing windows, grading articles, writing computer programs, or working on a home repair project. This high level of operation isn't just linked to adult jobs. It can be seen in the elementary school student who never fails a homework assignment, the high school student who has three extracurricular activities per day. The homemaker manages a household of three active children and community activities that fill every spare moment.

People with TMA react to their high-drive force, which can become a problem if it isn't channeled for the anxious mind's benefit. The high level of activity is unlikely to change, and people with TMA will never relax in the same way that a less motivated person would. Still, they may change how they focus their energy to find more harmony, more pleasure, and much less anxiety.

Work Style and Work Values

People who are incredibly involved do not consider their level of involvement to be a concern. Others may wish they were less busy, but they overlook an issue until it is brought to their attention. The pressure from a spouse or children to be more accessible may increase, especially if a family member has a problem that necessitates the person's time, such as when someone becomes ill and requires medical attention. When something prevents these high-drive people from functioning at their "usual" speed, they become irritated, and if the disruption lasts too long, their anxiety levels rise dramatically.

People with high drive are quickly thrown into anxiety when things do not go as expected, even though they are go-getters who get a lot done. Harry is an excellent example of this. He traveled for work regularly, and he almost always had a story about getting in trouble for hounding airline employees when flights were delayed or canceled. He struggled to reorganize his emotions in a way that would allow him to come up with a new solution or schedule for his time.

His anterior cingulate gyrus (ACG) was stuck, and he had trouble controlling his impulses. He appeared to be engaged outside, but he was disappointed with his failure to carry out a plan he had conceived inside. He couldn't quickly calm himself down in that state. Harry's anxiety was eventually under control after he came close to being arrested.

For people like Harry, being forced to stand still or stop working, whether for a short time or for a long time, will exacerbate their anxiety. When a meeting cancels, having an unexpected few free time hours can trigger anxiety about using it better. A stuck ACG can add to the anxiety by preventing the individual from seeking a suitable alternative use of the time. I got a call one morning from a client whose office had to close due to a plumbing problem.

The client was having a nervous breakdown about what to do for the day. He had so many ideas about what he could be doing that he couldn't even begin to pick the "right" one, and he knew that if he didn't make the most of his time, he'd become even more nervous. Anxiety can increase when an injury or illness slows you down. When work is disrupted by illness, people can attempt to return to work too quickly and relapse or even re-injure themselves, as I've seen with nervous clients recovering from surgery or a muscle or bone injury. Holding also seems to create a build-up of pressure that is difficult to release, and this pressure becomes a significant health and relationship issue. It may cause high blood pressure or irritability, as well as outbursts of frustration at

inopportune times or against people who do not
deserve it.

How to Control TMA

Why will someone suffering from TMA due to
anxiety be opposed to changing their habits or
activities? As a result of the increased exercise, anxiety
is reduced. When people aren't involved, they get
agitated, both psychologically and physically
distressing. When they sit still, particularly if they
haven't planned how they'll spend their free time,
their anxiety levels rise to an uncontrollable level.
TMA can be controlled using the strategies
mentioned below.

Prepare for the dreaded, unplanned "free" time. It is a
short tactic, but it is incredibly beneficial to the
overworked TMA. Life often throws up unforeseen
moments when people must standstill in some way.
People who fly for work are aware that they will
experience delays. They have no idea when the delays
will occur. Social activities may be canceled, leaving

you with an unwanted free afternoon or evening. People get sick, and work sessions are rescheduled, leaving a gap in the schedule. People with TMA cannot imagine what they would do if they ever had a spare minute, even though most people wish for a few extra hours to get things done.

They become trapped and unable to choose what to do with their "free" time because their anxiety spikes too quickly. They become concerned about making the right decision (choosing the wrong activity will be a mistake) and the passage of time and how well it would be spent. This condition necessitates a successful homework assignment.

1. Each time you say to yourself, at home or work, on the off chance that at any point, I have a couple of hours (or a couple of moments) to make a note. This activity can be anything by any means. Wash up, plant a nursery, arrange photographs, clean the carport, put together your devices, revamp your records, wipe out work area drawers, etc.

2. Transfer your note to the list you keep going. This list can be divided into three categories:
    - ✓ Things that take 30 minutes to complete
    - ✓ Things that take an hour to complete
    - ✓ Things that lasted 3 hours to complete
    - ✓ Things that take a day to complete

3. Keep a copy of the list on your person at all times, and if you have the dreaded unwanted "free" time, choose something from the list that matches the time you have. You'll know you wanted to do it, you'll be able to make a fast decision, and your anxiety will be eased.

4. Once you complete the tasks, cross them and add more to your notes folder. It is rewarding to people with TMA. If you're not a TMA person yourself, and you're supporting someone with TMA, don't underestimate how much this kind of problem—having unwanted free time—occurs and raises their anxiety. It is also likely that the TMA individual does not know these situations because of what they are. Be on the lookout when you hear about them.

This simple fix of preparation is, in reality, that: a simple fix for a regular and fully manageable worsening of anxiety in a highly active person. Identifying and Counter Perfectionism When people who are nervous sound like perfectionists, they also don't see themselves as perfectionists.

They don't feel wedded to something being fine as if order and correctness are priorities in themselves. Instead, perfectionism is a way to fend off anxiety for them, and they may not know it. What we see from the outside isn't what's going on inside. People with anxiety are trying to deal with it by removing the need to worry, and an excellent way to remove the need to worry is not to make any mistakes. The fewer mistakes they make, the less they're going to have to think about. And the effort to regulate the error becomes perfectionism. It sets them up to re-examine their work, double-check mistakes, work extra hours, and do their work instead of entrusting it to others.

Perfectionism is also showing up in social ways. The perfectionist can monopolize a committee on which they sit or refuse to allow others to carry out obligations, such as planning a party. Younger perfectionists will not trust anyone to participate in a school project. In all these situations, the underlying tendency is to take care of the situation and "do it better." It affects the relationship with other people who see the perfectionist as controlling.

What these perfectionists don't know is that no matter how hard they try, they will worry. They're just finding other things to think about, and their heightened tension makes them more hypervigilant and uptight. They also underestimate the repercussions of working too hard: nobody helps them anymore, they end up with more jobs, they start believing that they can do it all, and—wham! —their level of anxiety is even higher. It becomes a vicious cycle of searching for new issues to be avoided, locating them, being convinced that they have dealt with them, and continuing to look for more.

Jenny, an event planner (what an excellent work for her anxiety!), put it this way:

"I ask someone to take on a project. feel as if I can see how it will go, like dominos dropping." I can see the complete result if all goes well or how the dominos will fall if anything goes wrong. And I'm making a point of avoiding any potential trouble spots. That means that if I pay attention, nothing will go wrong. I enjoy anticipating problems so that I can be confident that everything will go smoothly and that everybody will be pleased."

When I asked why she was able to put in this amount of foresight and preparation to do all the planning herself, and she responded, "If I do it, then I won't have to think about it. If I were to let other people be responsible for parts of it, then I would stress until it was over. I might know something was going to go wrong, but I wouldn't know what it would be, and I would not be able to plan how to fix it. It is not worth the worry to let someone else do the work."

One way in which this anticipatory worry and perfectionism are advantageous is that perfectionists get strong positive reinforcement for being such successful workers. They get promotions and recognition and rewards, and good grades alleviating their concern about whether they are appropriate to others. It is a part of their lives they should feel good about.

On the other hand, they develop a paranoia that if they ever let down their perfectionistic guard, things will totally fall apart, and people will blame them entirely. (Note the extreme always/never expression. It is the way the thinking process goes.) In other words, they come to believe that everybody thinks errors are unacceptable and evidence of their unworthiness.

If you've got to get rid of a bad habit, what are you going to do? The first move is to recognize it. People who deal with anxiety in this way don't see themselves as perfectionists, so labeling them "perfectionists" isn't helpful at first. They consider themselves to be "caring" or "detail-oriented."

When working in therapy, it's essential to ensure that perfectionism isn't serving some implicit psychological purpose or resulting from a personality disorder like obsessive-compulsive disorder. These issues necessitate psychotherapeutic approaches that are beyond the reach of this technique. A thorough psychotherapy interview, such as using coherence therapy methods and a personality inventory, will help establish whether perfectionism has deeper psychological roots. On the other hand, perfectionism can be dealt with using anxiety management strategies if it is determined that it originated to combat anxiety.

Recognize perfectionism. It is a reasonably simple task. Look for hints in the person's language regarding work, family, and social obligations. The steps below will help you recognize perfectionism, which is often used to avoid anxiety but can lead to more anxiety if it isn't managed.

Do you feel a strong sense of personal responsibility for the outcomes of work, social, or family events, especially when other people might be expected to do some of the work? It would be most obvious in the primary areas of responsibility. If you're a student, you might see that in the way you participate in a club or committee, where you do all the work for the people who are supposed to be doing part of the planning. If you're a stay-at-home mom, you might not be able to rely on other family members to finish their laundry, clean your rooms or take the garbage out on time. There are several ways to see him at work—a project manager can take complete responsibility for the project's outcome in every aspect.

Is your language full of the extremes mentioned above? It is a strong indicator that the need to be perfect is linked to anxiety management. Take note of self-talk like, "This is terrible." "This staff never does things according to the manual." "No one around here really does what they say they will." "I still end up doing all the planning."

"If I don't get this done, the whole situation will be destroyed."

Do you have a sense of the difference between "good enough" and "great enough," and can you use it to decide how best to do it? Once these features have been observed, go on to search for a pattern.

- ✓ First, trace the past of this kind of action. Is there a time when you can recall that you didn't worry too much about the results?
- ✓ Next, think about what happens to the level of anxiety when something goes wrong. If your perfectionism is a way to avoid fear, your anxiety will go off the charts when you make a mistake.
- ✓ Take a look at the implications of your mistake/anxiety. Perfectionism grows as you overcome your fear by deciding whether to be more vigilant in the future or to take more information personally.

- ✓ Is there an escalating trend in which you experience less discomfort by taking care of situations and doing even more work, reviewing items more, or spending more hours on a task? If so, you might be using perfectionism as a way to fend off anxiety. Intervening on Perfectionism

Step 1. Find out the harmful effects of perfectionism. _This way of avoiding anxiety can be positive and can lead to self-esteem. Still, before you fully eradicate perfectionism as a shield against anxiety, you'll want to be sure that it has negative implications. Look for consequences, such as:_

- ✓ *Being accused (unfairly) of being overbearing rather than supportive or cautious.*
- ✓ *Taking extra jobs that no one asks you to do and feeling overworked.*
- ✓ *Feeling the burden of doing a job, feeling the strain of having no time for anything else, even time to have fun, which you sincerely believe*

you would have had if you could only find the time to quit working.

✓ A lack of satisfaction and enjoyment, even in activities that should be enjoyable, result from feeling responsible for the activity's outcome.

✓ You're tired and have no idea how or when you'll get up on your feet.

✓ You are not able to control the fear. It is a very crucial issue. If your perfectionism were helping you handle your anxiety, you wouldn't be struggling to suppress it. Why not stress less and find a different way to cope with anxiety? It is essential to strengthening the idea that letting go of excessive perfectionism would reduce anxiety levels in the long run. Other strategies for dealing with anxiety symptoms will reassure you and reinforce your ability to break the cycle.

Step 2: Exclude all/never language from your vocabulary. "Perfection is impossible" should be a motto for nervous perfectionists. "If anything is impossible, then I have no duty to search for it," you may add. Step 3: Make a non-perfectionism plan. Preparing for a less-than-perfect outcome of specific responsibilities is preferable to find an unintentional flaw. Since you'll be doing it on purpose, and you'll know you'll be able to handle the result, it won't be as stressful.

✓ Decide not to take on a particular, one-time responsibility to see how the job gets completed without you as part of your non-perfectionism preparation. In all seriousness, ask yourself, "How important is this?" Start tiny, but choose something you might have agreed to do anyway, such as mowing the lawn for someone who claims to be too busy, babysitting the grandkids, writing a report when someone else should, or covering someone else's change. The aim is to see how the job gets done even if you don't understand that someone else's urgency does not always imply value. You may find that if you hold back, someone else will take your place. Or, if the job isn't completed, it doesn't seem to be the end of the world.

✓ Pay attention to and analyze how people respond to others' shoddy work.

✓ Take some obligation but refrain from doing what others are supposed to be doing. Observe how the result affects other people's behavior and your anxiety level.

✓ Decide not to complete any tasks on which you might otherwise have worked yourself to death. Don't do something or miss a deadline by a few hours. You may need to seek guidance about what you should let go of, but go ahead and do it once you do. In others' minds, the types of circumstances that serve as good practice are generally minor—for example, don't go out to buy the right napkins for the party; instead, use paper towels. Alternatively, you might apply for a one-day extension on a project to see what your supervisor or instructor thinks. Alternatively, do not schedule the plan in advance of the staff meeting in writing. Most of the time, these kinds of detail-oriented things that you previously thought were important will turn out to be insignificant.

- ✓ Note how little someone cares whether you were accepted or not.
- ✓ Keep in mind that when something suddenly goes wrong, people (including yourself) usually handle it reasonably well.
- ✓ Finally, pay attention to what distinguishes valuable from insignificant items.

This evaluative phase will assist you in potential decisions on what you can eliminate and what you must keep. Your vision has been hazy when it comes to particular distinctions, and it will take some practice to clear it up.

Again, the way to recognize and fight perfectionism is to:

1. Look at the things you're trying to do correctly and listen to the words you're using.
2. Identify the vocabulary of extremes—"always or never" language.
3. Find a pattern of perfectionism in the style of work.
4. Identify the detrimental effects of perfectionism.
5. Start changing the vocabulary of extremes.
6. The plan for poor results.
7. Pay attention to results so that you learn to discern value from urgency and consistency from inconsistency. It will allow you to determine the trends in perfection properly.

Achieve Balance

Balance in life is threefold: maintaining emotional, physical, and mental wellbeing. People with TMA can accidentally get out of control, but they may not fix it. For example, someone might put all their effort into a hobby that's becoming addictive, like making crafts for sale at the Spring Fair. Another might make an effort to participate in his children's events, and yet another might become so focused on his job that he gives up all social interaction to spend more time in the office.

Getting out of balance is something that can sneak on a human. Sometimes, for a good reason, one aspect of life assumes importance over other pieces. It may be fair to work at your job 12 hours a day for a limited period when, for example, you are planning to sell your business or have your organization ready for inspection. It makes sense for someone to spend most of the nights in a single year completing his academic career at night school.

Shifting back to balanced operation, on the other hand, can be difficult for a TMA who has grown accustomed to the workload and continues to do so. These people can easily stay on the path they've set for themselves while other facets of their lives disappear from view. How much have you heard anyone asking, "I know I should exercise and look after my health, but..." "I know I should spend more time with my kids, but..." or "I know I should spend more time with my kids, but..." "I know it would be better if I took time for myself every day, but...." or "I know it would be better if I took time for myself every day, but...." These kinds of comments reveal the stress that comes with being out of balance—behaving in a way that goes against one's principles. High activity is not a benefit in and of itself, as the TMA individual quickly forgets.

Make a list of your time-related values.

It's challenging to start a conversation about a person's beliefs. There's not much debate about this in our society, but people respect their views, even though they haven't articulated them to themselves. "What do I do with my time?" you may wonder as a starting point for exploring life balance and whether it represents your values.

And though their significant others disagree, TMA people can be very good at convincing themselves that they are well-balanced. By presenting evidence, keeping an impartial, measurable record will put an end to the debate.

1. Keep track of what you do with your time for at least a week, every day, and for two weeks if the week does not reflect your life.

2. Draw a diagram. Divide the week into hours and each day into 15-minute time slots. To avoid deceiving yourself, fill in the chart each day, not at the end of the week.

   ✓ Make a list of all of your activities. Include everything from personal hygiene to television viewing and dining, as well as a rundown of work tasks.

   ✓ Add up how much time you spend on and task in minutes or hours and categorize it, such as work, children, social life, and so on.

   ✓ Construct a pie chart using the time totals from the chart.

Examine if your time management aligns with your values.

What is the appropriate time allocation for each activity? Is it reasonable to devote 8 hours to work, 2 hours to commuting, and 6 hours to other aspects of your life? What percentage of the 6 hours should be allocated to each of the other activities? It can be simple to make these choices, but it can be challenging to know when to make adjustments. Increasing time for something you want to do while taking time away from something that doesn't matter is the least stressful way to start changing the balance of time.

MANAGING THE ANXIOUS MIND PART 3

Technique 9: Implement a Plan and Practice

This approach focuses on developing competence and trust, which is the leading behavioral target for people who suffer from social anxiety symptoms such as being anxious in environments where they will be watched. Experiences that expand or improve expertise and ability are the only way to gain competence and trust.

Technique 10: Demonstrates how to gain competence and trust in dealing with anxiety at work and in social situations.

You'll need to use other strategies to develop a strategy and carry it out because part of trust is knowing that if anxiety arises, you'll be able to handle it.

Fear Is Learned and Unlearned By The Brain.

The expectation of being nervous triggers anxiety. People who have an enlarged amygdala (the part of the brain that alerts us when we're in danger) are likely to be excessively responsive to faces. The amygdala interprets even the tiniest change on a face as a negative, leading people to assume they are being judged as failures or that they will be rejected. Then they shape expectations like, "I can't talk in public without trembling and humiliating myself; if someone sees me eating, I'll humiliate myself in some way by spilling food or making a mistake. I know I'll panic if I have to wait a long time to be seated at the restaurant." The die has been rolled. They will panic or feel embarrassed if they are placed in such circumstances. Their aspirations shape Their future experience.

Fortunately, the amygdala, which alerts us to risk, also has a feature that allows us to unlearn our fear. However, it can only unlearn when placed in a condition that previously caused fear but no longer does. The cortex informs the amygdala that the current situation is secure, calming it and preventing it from fearing the future situation. If you've unlearned your apprehension, you'll be able to act competently and confidently in similar situations.

The amygdala would never be able to unlearn fear unless new learning is planned. You'll be filled with the same old extreme fear if you don't have a plan— your thinking brain will be preoccupied with noticing how frightening the situation is. Change necessitates a conscious decision to act as though the situation is not threatening. The amygdala will learn new things with careful planning and preparation.

Three Deep Breaths and Enough Preparation

When I was in high school, I extreme stage fright. I now know it was caused by panic attacks that appeared in various circumstances, including my acting. I used to pray to God to make me pass out before I had to go out and sing while waiting in the wings.

To be sure that death would not have been a highly effective avoidance strategy, but it was the best the rest of the cast and crew could come up with to ignore my cue. One of the best anxiety coping techniques I ever learned came from my drama coach: breathing slowly and deeply. She also helped me to develop a mental structure for dealing with my anxiety. "Three deep breaths and good planning are everything you need to go out there without fear." Her "three deep breaths and good preparation" method has been my go-to method for overcoming anxiety in any situation.

"three deep breaths symbolize the desire to stay physiologically relaxed while waiting for the exercise to begin." People who are going out into the real world and doing something new—ordering in a restaurant, speaking at a staff meeting, sitting in the center of a theatre, driving on the tollway—should keep as calm as possible so that their nervous responses are less likely to be triggered. An individual may choose to keep their body relaxed by breathing and relaxing their muscles, a prefrontal cortex activity that affects physiology and brain function.

Begin one-breath relaxation or your preferred breathing technique as soon as you realize a situation is likely to cause anxiety. You'll know you'll need it if you've prepared your practice ahead of time. If you're going to speak up at a staff meeting, for example, take a few deep breaths and relax during the day before the meeting. Avoid being tense and irritable. Once you're in the conference room, you'll use one-breath relaxation to keep yourself physically relaxed before it's your turn to talk. As a result, the body is kept as quiet as possible—the sympathetic nervous system and peripheral nervous system are both quieter—, and your symptoms are less likely to be caused. And if you are anxious, you will be less tense as you begin speaking and will be able to handle anxiety effectively, which is the ideal outcome of practice. Staying calm is an essential aspect of any planned exercise. Now that you know that, it's time to move on to strategy #10, creating a plan and practicing it in real life.

"Good preparation" refers to all stages of preparing to practice in real life as well as the actual practice session. Mental readiness, such as strategy #8 for improving self-talk, is part of the preparation process and serves as a mental bridge to practicing anxiety behavior management. Finding the right inspiration is also an essential part of good planning.

Why would someone who'd rather die than perform a solo to an audience go out and sing more than once? Inspiration is a powerful tool. I loved the act of singing until I was able to perform in front of an audience without dying. I'd practiced it and was confident in my abilities. Serotonin gave my brain a feeling of accomplishment for a job well done. As people cheered the results, dopamine flowed freely in my brain. An individual can overcome fear if they are motivated enough. Fear is reduced until it is confronted. With anxiety about performing well in charge, I majored in speech and drama in college.

Implement A Plan

Knowing just what you want in life and doing it is more complicated than most people believe. Remember what you want for a while, and then follow the steps below.

Set Goals

Setting a target is the first step in creating a plan. Goal-setting is what connects you to the drive to do the things that scare you. Keeping inspiration in front of you will help you face your fears and allow you to relax about them.

You're supposed to have a clear understanding of what you're doing. You want to do. People have a variety of objectives in mind, some of which are very particular and others which are more general:

- "Order without breaking a sweat in a restaurant."
- "Don't use a quavering voice while speaking to my boss."
- "This semester, stay in class."

+ "Start conducting work interviews."

The most effective strategies begin with being very precise about what you want to achieve.

Determine what makes you nervous and what skills do you require? What makes you nervous, and what skills do you require? Once you've decided on a target, you'll need to figure out what skills you'll need to achieve it. If you're going to a work event where you'll be greeting people and initiating conversation, evaluate your ability to do so comfortably. Assess the ability to answer interview questions if the aim is to go on a job interview. If you want to start dating again, consider what options you have for meeting people via email, phone, and in-person, as well as the communication skills you'll need.

A thorough examination of your past is needed to determine what makes you nervous and what skills you might need. It is very difficult to do on one's own. Working with a therapist during this process is not only beneficial but also likely required. Examine your life experiences in the areas below to determine what is needed.

Social Skills

Do you have a strong urge to socialize with your friends or date? Pockets of social insecurity can appear out of nowhere, and even the most well-adjusted individuals can have surprising insecurities about social activities.

Examine if you have acquired social skills for anything you want to do. Do you need to learn how to be assertive? Are you able to confidently introduce yourself to new people? What if you could walk into a conference room and choose where you want to sit or how you want to greet a colleague? Are you able to speak with your child's teachers or the parents of their peers in person or on the phone? Can you ask a new friend out on a date or invite them to a social gathering?

Do you have the skill and willingness to handle personal business's social aspects, such as signing checks or credit cards in front of a clerk or conversing with store employees? Can you ask questions when making a purchase, returning an item, or exchanging it?

Will you communicate with medical staff to explain medical conditions and treatments? Can you easily communicate with your child's coaches or tutors, schedule appointments, and make financial plans for lessons?

It is all about a job's social aspects, such as asking a boss's questions, talking with a coworker during a break, talking with a coworker about a work situation, etc. Is it possible to improve work-related and presentation skills? Is it possible to interview for a job? Do you know how to give a conference presentation? Do you know how to make a statement during a meeting of a committee? Do you have the ability to handle work-related conversations with bosses or supervisors?

Assertiveness is a trait that could be useful in all of these situations. In any case, assertiveness means understanding and being able to ask that your needs be heard and met. You were returning retail goods to a shop, objecting to false charges on a bill, asking a repairman to explain appointments or bills. Asking for changes in a job schedule or demanding a vacation date, and informing a boss that a work assignment is too much are all examples of cases where this is a valid concern.

Build Skills

Following the evaluation, the next step is to devise a strategy for improving skills and developing a practice schedule. When a person lacks skills, even simple skills, he or she is likely unaware of what skills are required or where to obtain them. That has to be meticulously prepared.

Skills can be taught in several ways. Workbooks can be used to teach social skills and assertiveness. In group counseling, you can learn assertiveness, social skills, dispute resolution, anger management, and other skills.

Community colleges' adult education departments also deliver free or low-cost courses on public speaking, flirting, interviewing, etiquette, and Internet communication. You might even enroll in an acting class!

Practice in Private

It's essential to practice the skills and make the steps small enough to be completed successfully. The brain requires victories to proceed to the next more challenging stage confidently. If you move too quickly, the brain can detect incompetence and cause fear. Breaking down each target into small steps is the best way to go. It's crucial to find the right instructor, who is usually a psychotherapist. The right amount of motivation is needed to learn new skills.

If you're working from a workbook, double-check that you've got the right idea and aren't moving too quickly, and a therapist will help you stay on track.

Mastering each level of competence will boost your faith in your ability to complete the task. If you want the amygdala to unlearn fear, you must not hurry into doing anything until you are confident you can do it. If you want to learn how to interview for jobs without being anxious, for example, you might break it down into smaller steps like these:

- Making a list of questions and referring to it casually while practicing asking the questions
- Learning to shake hands with eye contact and practicing this
- Gathering knowledge about your career experience, talents, and job skills and
- practicing explaining them verbally.
- Being able to pause and consider if a question calls for it without looking anxious
- Practicing job interviews with a therapist, friend, or coworker.

People can "act as if" with the help of a therapist. In other words, they will learn skills in a controlled environment as if they were in a real-life situation. Before going into practice in real life, the practice will help the amygdala unlearn some of the anxiety. An individual will try out skills that the therapist has taught them or skills they learn from workbooks during a therapy session. Another way to learn in private before going out into the real world is to enroll in a skills class.

Many people are unable to practice in private because they are ashamed. That is precisely why it is needed. It's the equivalent of preparing a part in a play and then declaring that you don't want to rehearse it before going onstage for the first time in front of an audience.

Practicing what you'll say to a restaurant waitress, what you'll say if you run into your new boss in the corridor. What you'll do if you need to use the toilet in the middle of a movie, what you'll say to your instructor if you don't think you'll be able to join a study group, and so on are all essential practice scenarios.

Find a partner to practice with—a parent, therapist, girlfriend, friend—or practice alone. If your lips have spoken the words before, they will remember them better. The amygdala, motor cortex, limbic system, anterior cingulate gyrus, orbitofrontal cortex, and prefrontal cortex all get a workout when you practice. And all parts of your brain are involved—the amygdala, motor cortex, limbic system, anterior cingulate gyrus, orbitofrontal cortex, and prefrontal cortex.

It will be easier to recall if you practice a lot. When you practice, you create circuits of connections in your brain that make it easier to remember what you've learned.

<u>To summarize:</u>

1. Make a specific target for yourself.
2. Determine what causes you to be nervous.

3. Develop your skills by reading and using workbooks, going to school, and so on.

4. Break it down into manageable chunks and complete them one at a time.

5. Work on your skills in private.

Desensitization of Trauma

Desensitization cannot be taught in this setting, but it must be discussed on behalf of those who have a history of trauma that prevents them from returning to a previous encounter.

Also, imagining a similar scenario may stimulate the sympathetic or peripheral nervous system in people who have been traumatized. In these cases, psychotherapy is needed to desensitize the trauma memory. On the other hand, panic creates a rapid connection between panic and the specifics of a case.

People who have panic attacks make the mistake of thinking the situation triggered the panic, and their minds then believe panic will happen again while they are in the situation. People who have panicked in a social environment will need assistance desensitizing before returning to a similar situation, just as people with social anxiety symptoms will need assistance recovering from shame trauma from circumstances in which they were too anxious and embarrassed for it.

Desensitization can be accomplished in three ways: systemic desensitization, energy therapy, and **EMDR**. Both of these techniques necessitate collaboration with a therapist who specializes in them.

- Desensitization in a systematic manner. The therapist starts by teaching the client relaxation and then creates a hierarchy of nervous elements. Starting with the factor that causes the least amount of anxiety, the client imagines it until he is fully relaxed. The therapist then takes the client up one step at a time before all components are desensitized.

- Energy healing. The client describes the thoughts that cause negative feelings and the nature of the negative feeling using this process (anxiety, embarrassment, phobia, etc.). She then assesses and scores the degree of negative physical arousal. She then taps on acupressure points that equate to physical arousal and scores the sensation again until the bad feeling is gone.

- EMDR (Eye Movement Desensitization and Reprocess For traumatic experience, particularly shame trauma for people with social anxiety, eye movement desensitization. And reprocessing (EMDR) is the most flexible, profound, and challenging approach for a therapist, but it also provides unattainable results with any other method. To use EMDR, therapists must be trained and certified.

In VIVO (Real-Life) Practice

In real life, rather than in private, it is conducted in small steps that gradually increase the amount of time spent in the situation, allowing a person to leave while still feeling relaxed. The steps should also shift from "low stakes" to "high stakes," with the latter reserved for ending the procedure rather than the beginning. For example, suppose someone afraid of sitting in the middle of a theater is practicing going to the movies.

In that case, he should not begin in vivo practice by arriving late, when the majority of the seats are already taken, and remaining for the entire film. He shouldn't go to a hit movie's opening night because every seat will be filled.

When the consequences of bolting from the theater in shame would risk humiliation in the eyes of a potential romantic partner, he could not invite a first date to accompany him on a practice run. Instead, this individual should break down the situation into increasing exposure measures, such as this:

1. Determine whether any skills, such as buying tickets without embarrassment, are needed.

2. Determine the duration of the exposure based on your level of anxiety and previous experience. Can you leave when the lights dim and people are already arriving and taking seats, or should you wait for the previews and then leave as if you need more popcorn before the show begins? If you're standing near the entrance, can you sit through a short film?

3. Decide if you'll need help from a friend or relative or whether it's easier (and less embarrassing) to go it alone.

4. Make the steps as big as possible while still being realistic. Arrive early for a show that has been running for a while. Sit on the aisle near the door and remain only as long as you intended. Leave feeling competent so that you can move on to the next stage of exposure with more confidence.

The most challenging aspect of this technique is determining the exact degree of exposure required to develop expertise without jeopardizing trust.

Cooperation for In Vivo Exposure

Obtaining the assistance of those who can help the exposure run more smoothly is a smart idea and a must. It is particularly true for anxious children about school. The principal, the school nurse, the students, and the counselor all need to be aware of the objectives of exposure to prevent unintentional escape or, worse, accidental embarrassment.

For younger children, parents play a crucial role. Madison, ten years old, had been anxious about school and was a shy girl, but she had friends, and her teacher liked her. She began requesting to stay home after seeing a substitute teacher twice a week, claiming she was sick in the mornings. (A person's stomach is a strong predictor of their level of anxiety!) Her parents let her stay at home "only until her stomach calmed down enough for her to return to school." Madison's troubled stomach only lasted for three days until she noticed that it always seemed to get better about 3 p.m. when school was out for the day, and she wouldn't have to go.

Her parents wanted to get her back into the class even though they knew she might scream, so they called the office to work out a plan.

Madison was supposed to go to school the next day, but she'd be able to leave early after the first two hours, which she liked. She'd stay later the next day, through lunch so she could sit with her best friend, and then leave when she was satisfied. On the third day, she'd spent the entire day with us. Madison's parents went over the proposal with her and double-checked that she was clear about everything.

They also double-checked that she knew what they had told her about breathing and remaining calm.

The design was started the next day. Madison's parents reached the classroom before the rest of the students, and the nurse and teacher welcomed them.

They explained that even though she was ill, the nurse would not call her parents and stay in the classroom and not go to the nurse if she screamed. Her parents reminded her that they would be there to pick her up after her second class as they exited the school. Madison screamed, but her avoidance behavior was not reinforced because no other students were present, and her parents were not present. She discovered that she did not feel ill despite being disturbed by the day's events in the classroom. Returning to school the next day was much better for both the parents and Madison.

Meagan, who was a freshman in high school, is another example. Meagan had always been a cautious person. Despite her strong performance in most subjects, she felt out of her depth in geometry. The instructor discussed it with her and her counselor after she formed a series of excuses to miss class, go home before class, and get sick right before class. Meagan admitted that speaking in math class was excruciatingly stressful for her. She couldn't bear the thought of being called upon, giving an incorrect response, and being embarrassed. <u>A strategy was worked out with her parents, the counselor, and the teacher:</u>

1. To remain calm in class, Meagan was taught one-breath relaxation.
2. Meagan's parents went over her homework regularly to practice saying the answers out loud.
3. The first-in-class in-vivo practice will take place the next day. If Meagan knew the answer, she would lift her hand. Her assignment was to do it at least once, preferably at the start of class. (This was the case of worry management using the "do the worst first" method.)
4. If her hand were up, the teacher would automatically call on her; if it were not, the teacher would not call on her.
5. When Meagan completed each step, she would discuss her accomplishments with her parents and advisor and then proceed to the

next step in class. <u>**The next stages of practice would take place as soon as Meagan felt competent to raise her hand and get called on immediately:**</u>

- Meagan would raise her hand, and the teacher would either call her or not, helping her get used to being called "surprise."
- As she waited, she would practice one-breath relaxation.
- The next step would be attempted until she felt confident in her ability to wait without being anxious.
- When her hand was up in class, the instructor would only call on her once.
- The final stage will be for Meagan to solve a homework issue on the board until she was confident in her ability to do so. The instructor will inform her ahead of time about the issue for which she would be responsible.

Practice Without a Support Person

Adults may have social interests that do not necessitate collaboration with others, but when they live with others, there is typically someone who acts as a buffer for them when it comes to things they need to avoid. If a partner or parent is involved, make sure they know the strategy and do not unintentionally thwart it.

Jerrold had just been named project manager for a contract his company was about to start. He was now in charge of providing daily reports in meetings he had never had to attend before. Although he was unconcerned about speaking with his team—they understood him well. It felt more like a conversation—attending meetings with the manager and other directors made him nervous. When Jerrold devised his strategy, the aim was precise: he wanted to talk in front of his bosses without turning red and sweating. His ability to hold a conversation was adequate; however, he had avoided speaking in front of a group for so long that he had no idea how to deal with the pressure. He'd been to more meetings than he could remember, and he'd listened to a lot of reports. However, he'd still been so preoccupied with his discomfort and avoidance methods that he hadn't paid attention to how other people treated themselves as they interjected remarks or gave reports. What happened in meetings and what he feared would cause his anxiety needed to be assessed.

1. Jerrold began by observing the meetings, paying attention to how people introduced themselves, got coffee, and settled into their seats. He was supposed to follow the procedure for people reacting to a report. How were people recognized, summoned, or referred to? He intended to enter the room before observing how people entered, greeted one another, and how the meetings progressed. His task was to listen in on other people's conversations.

2. Jerrold took the next step by making a list of his findings and identifying his self-talk about each one. He discovered a series of negative self-statements, including, "I'll never be as relaxed as Morgan," "No one will listen to me because I'm not charming like Frank," and "I'll turn red the minute someone looks at me, and my reputation will be fired."

3. He then created a list of counter-cognitions to help him psychologically plan.

4. Finally, before giving his first full report, he made a list of steps he needed to practice.

Jerrold used the concepts we had identified to increase the level of exposure gradually. It was growing exposure to being looked at without feeling on the spot in this case. He realized that his habit of being the first one in the room before a meeting was a form of avoidance. As a result, he had avoided having to deal with being scrutinized when he entered a meeting.

1. Jerrold wanted to practice entering the room later and later before he could do so without feeling claustrophobic. Over a few weeks, he was able to do this.

2. He realized that he had overestimated the amount of attention he received when he checked his progress. He felt better after that.

3. He decided to practice making remarks when he would have otherwise remained silent. He chose to begin by making brief statements that showed his agreement with an argument, so he wouldn't be worried about starting a fight.

4. He noted that people were respectful to him and acknowledged his suggestions as he assessed his performance.

5. His final practice was to locate a debated subject and make a statement in favor of one side of the argument. To his delight, he had no trouble finding an opening because every meeting included back-and-forth dialogue.

6. In assessing his accomplishments, Jerrold noticed that he was expecting everyone to

pounce on him if he expressed an opinion but that everyone else was doing so. No one seemed surprised when he did.

7. He was eager to plan and deliver his first paper, which he had practiced many times out loud to ensure he understood what he was going to say.

Jerrold followed the principles of good real-life practice:

- Write down a list of short, doable measures.
- Increase the time of exposure and the speed of the measures. That means extending your time in a situation, speaking for more extended periods, interacting with more people, and so on.

What Happens If I Miss a Step?

The aim of breaking down a plan into small steps is to increase the likelihood of success. However, you can encounter times when you are unable to complete a move. When this happens, don't be discouraged or give up! Keep in mind:

+ The in vivo procedure reveals additional information. The good news is you know what to expect if something goes wrong.
+ Everybody makes mistakes at some point. No one is excluded.

You are an individual.

+ If you don't get what you want in the first move, it's not a big deal.; you've been scared or humiliated before and survived it. It's second nature to your brain.

There will be a chance to try a different approach once more.

Help from Medication

Although these procedures are meant to be performed without drugs, a word of caution is required here. Only in this situation—real-life practice—can use medicine to keep calm be a clear benefit to learning. When people are overcome by anxiety, they are unable to learn new things. When they are training, it is essential to keep their nervousness or anxiety at a manageable level. Since panic, flushing, sweating, and trembling are so challenging to avoid entirely, having medicine as a back-up to minimize the level of anxiety during practice can be extremely beneficial.

Some of my clients make a strategy for their doctor to use their anti-anxiety drugs on an as-needed basis while trying something new. They are still anxious, but it is much less intense, and they are much more likely to manage their anxiety and complete their move successfully. The amygdala can unlearn fear in that situation due to this, and hope is established that the next move would also function. One trial without medication before going on to the next phase is a safe idea. After that, you can use it for the first trial of the next small move. **To summarize the steps of in vivo exposure, they are as follows:**

1. Remember the rule of "three deep breaths and good planning." This aids in the relaxation of the mind and body, setting goals, and acquiring skills.

2. Make a list of all the small steps that could be taken and pick the one that is the most difficult to complete.

3. Enlist the aid of those who can support or unwittingly obstruct the measures to ensure that they grasp the plan and work for you rather than against you.

4. Determine when medicine will be used and the first trials of the graduated measures.

5. Begin scheduled, graduated real-life practice steps—specific minor steps that can be practiced for which progress is ensured by private practice and faith in calm-down skills.

6. Assess the progress and choose the next step, extending the time of exposure while ensuring that the step can be completed so that new learning can take place.

7. Evaluate any mistakes to complete the steps and make practice course corrections.

8. Continue to prepare for each move until the entire target is achieved. The new learning (or unlearning of fear) at each point lays the

groundwork for the next move to take place safely. The safe experience will not entirely turn off the alert signal for that particular scenario in the future until the entire target is reached.

CONCLUSION

What the practice is all about is doing practice runs to do something you haven't been able to do before. No one heads out for a practice run without having done their homework. When you're training for an athletic event, you learn new skills, practice them, see what works and what doesn't, get guidance on how to do them, and then practice them again before the game. When training for a marathon, you begin with short runs and gradually build-up to the long run. If you're going to act in a play, you'll need to practice reading lines from a script and remaining inside the lines drawn on the floor to indicate where the stage is. Then you practice without the script on stage, and then you have a dress rehearsal of all of the parts in order before you perform in front of an audience. In vivo research follows the same rules. Develop the ability to take three deep breaths, plan ahead of time, and prepare to face reality. It is possible with practice.